The *Life* of John Calvin

John Calvin

The *Life* of John Calvin

Theodore Beza

EVANGELICAL PRESS

EVANGELICAL PRESS
Grange Close, Faverdale North Industrial Estate, Darlington,
Co. Durham, DL3 0PH, England

First published in Geneva in 1564
Revised and enlarged edition published 1657
Modern French version published 1993 by Editions Europresse,
Chalon sur Saône, France
This translation first published 1997

British Library Cataloguing in Publication Data available

ISBN 0 85234 404 X

Printed and bound in Great Britain by Creative Design and Print
Wales, Ebbw Vale

Contents

Theodore Beza

Theodore Beza, the author of this biography of Calvin, was born in Vézelay, in northern Burgundy, in 1519 into a noble family, several members of which held important positions in society. Some ten years younger than Calvin, he grew up in comfortable circumstances and as a young man frequented the court of Francis I of France.

What distinguished Beza from the other noblemen, however, was the fact that he had been taught by some of the best teachers of his day and had gained a profound knowledge of philosophy, law and the classics. In particular, he studied for some years under the German Melchior Volmar, an able teacher who also taught Calvin Greek. Beza lodged for a time with the Volmar family, but returned to Paris when they left for Germany.

It is easy to imagine the kind of life a young man of noble birth, who was handsome, rich and well educated and moved in fashionable circles, would have led in the French capital. Everything in his personal circumstances conspired to lead him into a frantic pursuit of worldly pleasure.

Beza, who was very keen on poetry, gave himself up to a life of enjoyment and in time fell in love with a young girl named Claudine Denosse. This young woman was modest and virtuous and Beza encountered a resistance on her part such as he

Theodore Beza

was unused to receiving. Spurred on by her rejection of his advances, he made concessions and married Claudine, but in secret because of the difference in rank between them.

Some time later he succumbed to a serious illness from which he nearly died. The long hours of enforced inactivity during his illness gave him ample time for some soul-searching which proved most salutary. His wife's devotion, the memories of the godly teaching that he had received in the Volmar household and reading a work by the Reformer Henry Bullinger all made him come to see life in a different way. He was overcome with remorse at the thought of the futility of his past way of life.

It was at this time that he resolved that in future he would be guided by the precepts of the gospel, for a real change had been brought about in his heart by the power of the Holy Spirit. He vowed that from then on he would proclaim the truth of God. However, to carry out such a resolve in France at that time amounted to pronouncing one's own death sentence. So in 1549 Beza renounced his privileges, his wealth and hopes of future advancement and, accompanied by his wife, set off for Switzerland.

He lived for ten years in Lausanne, where he taught Greek and began writing. In 1559 he was appointed principal of the Geneva Academy and a pastor of the church in that city. On Calvin's death Beza succeeded him and carried on the work of reformation in Geneva until his own death in 1605.

In Calvin and Beza, God's providence brought together two men of very different characters and backgrounds and united them in a common purpose, to the praise of the glory of his grace which was so evidently at work in the sixteenth century.

The Publishers

Author's preface

Note: This life of Calvin appeared in print for the first time in the form of an introduction to the last of his published works, the *Commentary on Joshua*, which was published at Lyons in 1564 by Theodore Beza.

If it had pleased God to keep his faithful servant, Mr John Calvin, among us for a longer time — or, rather, if the Lord had not been impelled by the corruption of the world to take him to himself so soon — then this commentary would not have been the last of his works.

In his books, Calvin faithfully devoted himself to promoting the glory of God and building up the church, and he was successful in achieving these aims. Even today, had its author still been alive, this commentary would not have seen the light of day without being adorned with a fine preface, as were the others in the past. But in this respect it resembles poor orphans, who enjoy less privileges than their older brothers as a result of the premature death of their father. Yet, thanks be to God, I see that this latest addition to his works comes of such good pedigree and displays such clear evidence of his authorship that I have no fears that it needs any further testimonials to make it, not only acceptable, but also profitable to all who read it.

Nor has it been my intention to recommend this book through my own testimony (what need is there for that?), but rather to join with it in lamenting the death of the man who has been like a father to both of us. I cannot, and indeed ought not to, regard the one who taught me any less as a father than this book should fail to acknowledge the authorship of the one who wrote it.

So, then, I will mourn him, yet not without a measure of consolation. Indeed, I would have had far too little real love for the man I am speaking of during his lifetime here below, if the knowledge that he has now been received into eternal bliss did not transform grief over my own loss into rejoicing at his gain. I would also have profited very little from his teaching, which was so godly and so worthy of admiration, or from his upright and blameless life, or from his peaceful death as a Christian, if I had not learnt through all these means to submit to God's providence and be completely satisfied and content.

However, in order that all those who loved and honoured him — whether through meeting him, or reading his works, or from what they have heard about him — might join me in finding grounds for comfort in God for this loss, I have written a very simple account of his life and death. Both will serve to refresh their memories of his teaching. This narrative will also help to silence those malicious men who speak ill of him and swamp the people who know no better with false rumours and slanders.

It is true that Calvin's writings, and the reputation that their author gained among us over the last thirty years, speak for themselves and are enough to frighten the malicious men who want to invent all kinds of accusations against him. These men might even feel some sense of shame over their actions if they had an ounce of decency left in them.

But we are not unaware of the excessive spitefulness displayed by many today, even among those who have had some experience of the knowledge of the gospel. They do not have a guilty conscience about slandering believers or defaming God's servants, for they always find some who are prepared to listen, and even claim to believe it all, even while knowing that these reports are all lies.

Finally, I also want to provide answers for those simple souls who have let themselves be led astray by false rumours that are all too easy to believe. These lies have discouraged many of them from reading Calvin's books.

To sum up, all will see from this narrative how the story of this man's life shows him to be a person who was, in the mercy of God, raised up and marked out to be a worthy servant in his church. The Lord, in his own time and place and through the means of his own choosing, called him by pure grace alone. Then he led him on, strengthened him and enabled him to persevere in the way of holiness until the day of his death, so that he might edify God's people by his preaching and his writings, and by a life lived in conformity with the truth.

Theodore Beza

1.
The early years

For the sake of simplicity I will keep to the chronological order of events, pausing where necessary to refer to people or places that will help to enhance our understanding of this account.

My narrative therefore begins with the birth of John Calvin, which took place on 10 July 1509. I do not attach any special significance to this date, as if we could hope to find in his horoscope an explanation for any of the events of his life — far less for his excellent personal qualities. I am simply stating a historical fact.

Indeed, Calvin himself was deeply horrified by the abuses involved in the so-called 'laws of astrology'. He published a book on this very subject, in which he demonstrated forcefully and in great detail, basing his arguments firmly on the Word of God, that such things should not be tolerated in the church or in a well-ordered society. He saw all such astrology as a lie and a complete waste of time. We should therefore be doing him a grave injustice if we were to indulge in speculations of this nature concerning his own life and personality.

Suffice it therefore to say that God, wanting to use his servant at a time which his holy wisdom had appointed, brought him into the world on the date mentioned above.

John Calvin was born in Noyon, a famous old town in the province of Picardy. He had four brothers. His older brother,

Charles, survived to adult life but died some time after their father. Antoine, the youngest, who outlived him, was his constant companion over a period of twenty-eight years. Two other brothers, François and another Antoine, both died young.

Calvin himself was christened John and his sponsor for the sacred rite of baptism was a canon of Noyon called Jean des Vatines. In later life Calvin would often refer to his baptism in order to illustrate the clear distinction which must be made between man-made traditions and the ordinance divinely instituted by the Lord Jesus Christ himself. He would say, 'I renounce the chrism [i.e. the consecrated oil used for anointing] but stand by my baptism.'

His father, Gérard Calvin, came originally from a nearby town called Pont-l'Evêque, but had lived in Noyon almost all his life. His wife's name was Jeanne le Franc. The family were well respected and enjoyed a comfortable standard of living, since Gérard's services as a notary were highly sought after in the households of the local nobility on account of his sharp mind and sound judgement. Because of his contacts he was able to arrange for his son John to receive a first-class education, studying alongside the children of the Montmor family, though at his father's expense. When the Montmor boys went to Paris to continue their studies, John accompanied them.[1]

On his arrival in the capital, Calvin began by attending the Collège de la Marche, where one of his tutors was Mathurin Cordier, a plain, unaffected man of good character who took his duties very seriously. This man subsequently devoted his whole life to teaching children, not only in Paris but also at Nevers, Bordeaux, Neufchatel, Lausanne and, finally, Geneva, where he died on 8 September 1564, at the age of eighty-five. He was still teaching his first-year class up to three or four days before his death.

COURT OF HOUSE AT NOYON, WHERE CALVIN WAS BORN.

Calvin's family home at Noyon

Calvin next went to the Collège de Montaigu, where he studied under a Spanish tutor who went on to become a doctor of medicine. The young lad had a lively, enquiring mind which enabled him to take full advantage of the tuition he received and to make rapid progress in the study of philosophy. In his conduct he gave evidence of being highly conscientious, strongly opposed to all the vices and devoted to what was believed at that time to be the service of God.

His heart inclined towards the study of theology, and his father expected to be able to find him employment in the church. With this object in view, Gérard obtained for his son a post at Noyon Cathedral.[2] John Calvin was also given a curacy at Pont-l'Evêque, his father's home town. He preached there on several occasions before leaving France.[3]

Although his father had originally intended that John should enter the church, he subsequently decided that his son should study law instead, seeing this as a better means of gaining wealth and status. In the meantime, through the influence of a close relative named Pierre Robert (who was given the surname Olivétan[4] and was a translator of the Bible into French) John Calvin himself had already come to know something of a purer form of religion and was beginning to be disillusioned with the superstitions promulgated by the papacy.

This fact, combined with the great respect in which he held his father, led him to agree to embark upon the study of law rather than pursuing a career in theology, especially as the theological schools of those days were extremely corrupt. He therefore made his way to Orleans, where an excellent man named Pierre de l'Estoille was teaching law at that time. This man was later appointed as presiding judge of the parliamentary court in Paris.

Under l'Estoille's tuition, Calvin made such rapid progress that he was often taken for one of the regular teachers rather

The Collège de Montaigu

than just a student. In fact, he spent more time teaching than studying. He was offered a post as a teacher, but turned it down.

At that time the University of Bourges had an excellent reputation due to the fact that Andreas Alciati, a renowned professor of law, was teaching there. Calvin therefore decided to go to Bourges to see and hear this man for himself.

All this time he had not neglected the study of Holy Scripture. On the contrary, he studied the Bible to such good effect that even at this early stage all those whose hearts God had touched with a desire for a purer form of religion viewed him with great affection and were filled with admiration for his evident scholarship and zeal for the things of God.[5]

He also worked hard at his university studies and there are still trustworthy men alive today who were on intimate terms with him at Orleans and who can testify that he often stayed up till midnight to study and ate hardly any supper in his eagerness to press on with his work. Each morning when he woke, he would stay in bed for a few moments while he recalled to mind all that he had studied the previous day and mulled over it, so to speak.

He kept these late hours so that he could devote himself more freely and without risk of interruption to his principal studies. I am convinced that these hours spent in study laid the foundation for his profound scholarship in the study of Holy Scripture, and helped him to develop the remarkable powers of memory which were to be so evident in his later life. But there is no doubt that these long hours and late nights seriously damaged his health.

During his time in Bourges, he frequently spent time in the company of Melchior Volmar, a man of excellent qualities. Volmar was of German nationality and was a teacher of Greek in the employment of the Duchess of Berry, who was later to become the Queen of Navarre. I have special memories of him for he was a faithful tutor and mentor to me in my younger days — something I will thank God for all my life.

This good man, seeing that Calvin's knowledge of Greek left much to be desired, enthusiastically set about perfecting his knowledge of that language. In this he was doing Calvin a good turn, as his pupil was later to acknowledge when he dedicated his commentary on the Second Epistle of Paul to the Corinthians to Melchior Volmar, describing him as his 'master'.

At this time Calvin used to preach occasionally in a small town in the Berry region called Lignières, where the lord of the manor welcomed him into his house. This man, who had only a limited understanding of things, used to say that he thought Mr John Calvin a better preacher than the monks and that he went straight to the heart of the matter in a way that they did not. This nobleman was not by nature a particularly superstitious man and he was well aware that the monks who came to the town to preach were feigning poverty to acquire a reputation for holiness or in the hope of obtaining some kind of material gain.

It was while he was in Bourges that Calvin heard the news of his father's death. This prompted him to abandon his law studies and return to Noyon. From there, he set off once again for Paris. In 1532, during his stay in the French capital, he wrote a learned *Commentary on Seneca's Book concerning the Virtue of Clemency* which is worthy of note. He was only twenty-four years old at the time. In spite of his youth, he was already well known and was honoured by all those who had any love for the truth.

2.
The road to Geneva

Of all the acquaintances that he made in Paris, Calvin always treasured the memory of a wealthy merchant called Etienne de la Forge, who was a God-fearing man. La Forge was burnt at the stake for the cause of the gospel in January 1535, and Calvin refers to him in the fourth chapter of his book against the Libertines.[1] Whenever he spoke of this man, he would bear witness to his godliness, to his simple, unaffected manner and the total absence of any duplicity in his character. He presented him as a very prudent, hard-working man of business who was none the less able to maintain a clear conscience and a consistent Christian witness.

Calvin himself, having resolved to dedicate himself wholly to God from then on, was achieving excellent results in his work — so much so that, when a riot broke out in Paris while a man called Nicolas Cop was rector of the university, Calvin was sent to plead his cause before the court. He achieved recognition for his involvement in this case and was well received by all who had any wish to see right and justice prevail in such matters.

The cause of the unrest related to the sermon preached by the rector already mentioned, Nicolas Cop, on the occasion of the festival of All Saints' Day, according to the custom of the time. In this sermon he had spoken out about questions of

Calvin as a young man

religion with a degree of boldness and openness that the Sorbonne and Parliament were not prepared to tolerate.

The parliamentary court sent for Cop to appear before them. He, for his part, was already on his way to court, accompanied by his vergers. However, when he received a warning that imprisonment awaited him, he did not go to the palace but returned home. He then left France for his home town of Basle, where his father, Guillaume Cop, enjoyed great renown as the royal physician.

As a result of his connection with Cop, Calvin too was obliged to leave Paris. Morin, the bailiff, even went so far as to search his room at the Collège de Fortet, with the intention of taking him prisoner. When Calvin was not to be found, Morin seized everything in the way of books and documents that he could lay his hands on. Among these papers were several letters from friends in Orleans and elsewhere, and the bailiff attempted to use this correspondence to make trouble for the people concerned. However, God prevented him from carrying out his plans.

From Paris, Calvin went to live in Saintonge, where he lodged with Louis du Tillet, a young man from a wealthy family who held office in the church.[2] This friend asked his guest to set down in writing a number of sermons and brief messages of Christian exhortation. Du Tillet arranged for some of the local priests to recite these writings in the course of the parish mass, in order to awaken in the people a desire for a true understanding of the doctrine of salvation through Jesus Christ in all its purity.

While he was living in Saintonge, Calvin travelled to Nérac to meet Jacques Lefèvre d'Etaples, a good man, now well on in years, who had formerly been tutor to the royal children. He had retired to the region of Gascony because of persecution from the Sorbonne. The worthy old gentleman was overjoyed to see Calvin and to spend time in discussion with him.

Some time later, Calvin left Saintonge and returned to Paris. At first he did so anonymously as the capital could offer him no security. However, Michael Servetus was just then beginning to spread his heretical teaching in the city and Calvin agreed to meet him in the hope of silencing him, or of convincing and reproving him from the Word of God.[3] To that end they arranged to meet at an agreed time at a house on the rue Saint-Antoine. Calvin kept the appointment despite the risk he was running by so doing, but Servetus did not turn up, although the others waited a long time in the hope that he would come.

Finally, in view of the low state to which religious affairs had sunk in the kingdom of France, Calvin decided to leave, so that he could live as his conscience directed without constant harassment. He therefore left the country in the year 1534, accompanied by Louis du Tillet, his young friend from Saintonge whom I mentioned earlier.

Before his departure, while he was staying for a time in Orleans, he wrote a book called *Psychopanychia*, on the subject of what happens to the soul after death. In it he refuted the false teaching of those who claimed that, after its separation from the body, the soul sleeps until the Day of Judgement. This work demonstrates the skill Calvin had by now acquired in expounding Scripture.

To leave France, Calvin and his companion travelled through Lorraine and arrived in Basle. Along the way, the despicable behaviour of one of the two servants they had taken with them caused them a great deal of trouble. At a place called Delme, in the vicinity of Metz, the man stole the purse containing all their money and made off with one of their horses. This theft would have left them in dire straits had not their other servant (who is still alive at the time of writing) put at their disposal the ten crowns he had on him. This enabled them to reach Strasbourg and from there they travelled on to Basle.

When he had been living in this town for some time Calvin had the first edition of his *Institutes* printed. It was in the form of an apologia addressed to King Francis I on behalf of the poor believers who were suffering persecution. In fact the King of France was wrongly labelling these people as Anabaptists so that his persecution of the gospel would not be condemned by the Protestant princes of Europe.[4] Calvin mentions this fact in the preface to his commentary on the Psalms.

This is an appropriate point to mention that, in his concern to pursue his studies, both in Basle and in Strasbourg, Calvin applied himself, among other things, to learning the Hebrew language. He made rapid progress in this field and his writings bear witness to the fact that it has since proved a great help to him in his understanding of Scripture.

Platter's printing-house at Basle where the *Institutes* were printed

Leaving Basle, Calvin travelled on to Italy accompanied by his friend du Tillet. He stayed for some time in Ferrara, where he met the Duchess of Ferrara (who, in the goodness of God, is still living).[5] After meeting Calvin and hearing what he had to say, this lady appreciated the true state of affairs and this excellent servant of God has occupied a high place in her esteem and affections ever since.

From Italy, the two men returned to Basle. Some time later Calvin left Basle to visit France. Meanwhile Louis du Tillet came first to Neufchatel and then to Geneva. Once Calvin had set his affairs in order at his old home, he planned to return to Basle and then to Strasbourg. This time he took with him his brother Antoine, who has already been mentioned.[6]

Because of the various wars that were going on, the most direct route was closed. Fortunately this meant that he passed through the town of Geneva. This city had shortly before made a stand for the gospel, thanks to the preaching of two outstanding servants of God, William Farel and Pierre Viret. Calvin did not plan to stay long in the town, but simply to pass through without stopping any longer than necessary.

However, du Tillet, who had followed him to Basle and then to Italy, made Calvin's presence in the city known. Du Tillet had in fact settled in Geneva, as had M. Morlet, who later became the king's ambassador to the Catholic League. The latter died several years later in Basle, but he always remembered his time in Geneva and he never passed through Lausanne or Geneva without wanting to see Calvin and Viret and have a talk with them.

The Lord, who was already preparing the way for all the rich blessing that he planned to pour out on his church through the instrumentality of Calvin, laid it on Farel's heart to keep him here in Geneva. Persuading him to stay proved particularly difficult, so much so that when entreaties failed to move him it was necessary to resort to solemn warnings. Farel threatened that if he refused to devote himself to the Lord's work in the church here in Geneva, God would put a curse on the tranquil refuge he sought to find in his studies. Calvin gave in and agreed to stay in Geneva. However, he stipulated that he would only teach theology and not take on the duties of a minister of the Word.

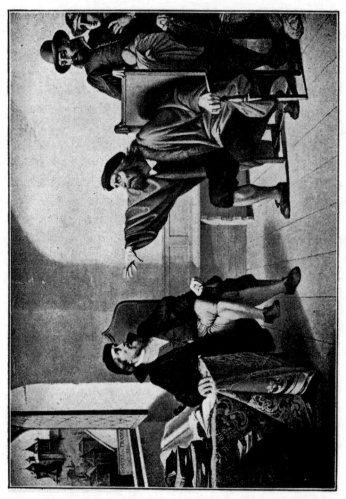

Farel persuades Calvin to stay in Geneva
(from the painting by J. L. Lagardon)

3.
Early conflicts lead to expulsion from Geneva

The events just related, which led John Calvin to settle in Geneva, took place at the beginning of September 1536. A year later, Calvin was also appointed as pastor. Now that he had been officially designated as a pastor and teacher of this church, by means of a lawful election and with the consent of the membership, he drew up a brief confession of faith and articles of church discipline in order to give some kind of structure to this newly formed church. He also compiled a catechism — not the one in use today, which consists of a series of questions and answers, but rather a simple résumé of each of the central points of the faith.

Believing that it was a sign of disrespect for the sacraments to allow people to partake of the Lord's Supper when it was not known whether or not they had renounced the idolatry and superstitions associated with the papacy, Calvin and his companions required the city magistrates to call the people, in groups of ten at a time, to pledge their adherence to the confession of faith. This request met a favourable response and, under orders from the Council, the people willingly complied. Calvin refers to this in a preface to a Latin edition of the catechism mentioned earlier, which he had printed in Basle in 1538.

This good beginning greatly angered Satan and his followers. Discontented as they already were as a result of the earlier political and religious changes which had been adopted in the town, they were bound to stir up opposition.

Barely four months had passed before Calvin found himself under attack, on one hand from the Anabaptists (one of whose number, Jean Stordeur, we shall hear of again) and, on the other, from an evil apostate named Pierre Caroli, who was a professor in Paris. The latter, who had the secret support and backing of a number of the most important citizens, had the potential to cause Calvin a great deal of trouble.

As for the Anabaptists, Calvin was so successful in refuting their teaching in the course of a public debate (in which the magistrates took no part) that this party ceased to have any influence in the church at Geneva. This is all the more remarkable when we consider that most churches in Germany are still infected with this teaching. In general, those which are now free of it only achieved this by invoking the full powers of the law, rather than by other means.

Space does not permit me to recount all the details of the long and bitter struggle over the slanderous allegations made by Caroli[1] in which not only Calvin but William Farel and Pierre Viret were also involved. Suffice it to say that Caroli was condemned by two synods — those of Lausanne and Berne. He held pastorates in these areas and had also married. However, he went to see the Cardinal of Tournon and, with the cardinal's help, obtained a letter of pardon from the pope. He changed sides in this way several times, vacillating between the papacy and the gospel.

Finally, after several clashes with Calvin, both in public debate and in writing, and after being expelled from the church of God, this wretched man died in miserable circumstances in a hospice in Rome. His example should serve as a warning to those who rebel against Jesus Christ to follow a master who rewards his servants so poorly, both in this world and the next.

In the year 1537, Calvin published two letters which he had written to some of his friends in France during his trip to Italy. In one he urges his readers to flee from idolatry and to conserve the purity of the Christian religion. The other discusses whether a Christian man should hold office within the church of which the pope is head or whether he should resign his post.

Around this time there were a number of revolts in the town, one after the other, which were a cause of much concern and grief to Calvin. There were even those who rose up in protest against the evangelical form of worship despite the fact that all the inhabitants of the town had formally adopted it under oath.

Calvin showed real heroism in his vigorous and unwavering opposition to the rebels. He was supported in this by Farel and by another worthy man called Courauld, who, like Calvin, was a minister at the church in Geneva. This man was blind as far as his physical sight was concerned, but in the spiritual realm he had great discernment. Calvin had brought him to Geneva from Basle, where he had fled from the fierce persecution raging in France.

The Lord was working out his purposes through this confrontation in a number of ways. In particular it was his plan to withdraw his servants from the scene of these difficulties, to rid the town of certain rebels who were giving the gospel a bad name, to establish a witness to his name elsewhere and, finally, to form the character of his servant through experiences which were to stand him in good stead in later life.

The majority of the Council were not on the side of justice. Consequently, the ministers of the gospel were ordered to leave the town within three days because of their refusal to hold the Lord's Supper and the trouble that this caused in the town.[2]

When he received the order to leave Geneva, Calvin commented that if he had only been serving men then he would have been poorly rewarded for all his trouble. But he was a servant of the one who, far from failing to reward his servants properly, gives them far more than they deserve. He was entitled to speak in this way, for he had followed the example of the apostle Paul in serving the church at his own expense.

So, to the great regret of all those whose hearts had been moved by the gospel, Calvin left Geneva and made his way first to Basle. From there he was called to Strasbourg, where he was welcomed as a precious addition to their number by such worthy men as Bucer, Capito, Hedio and others, who at that time were shining lights and pearls of great price in the church of God.

With the permission of the governors and other influential citizens of Strasbourg, Calvin founded a French church there in which he established a system of church discipline, something which the Germans have never yet been able to achieve for their church. He also gave lectures in theology, which were greatly admired by all and sundry, and for this he was paid an appropriate salary by the local authorities.

After Calvin's departure there were some in the church at Geneva who wanted to change the custom which had prevailed in the church up till that time of using ordinary bread for the Lord's Supper. They proposed, without any good reason, that wafers like those used in the mass should be used instead. This created real difficulties for some of the true believers, causing them to abstain from the Lord's Supper and to complain about the change. Some even were obliged to leave the town.

Calvin got wind of what was happening. While he personally did not see the point of making changes without good reason, he strongly warned those who stood for the gospel against the folly of taking offence over such a trivial matter. In fact, after he was settled back in the church at Geneva, and during the remaining twenty-three years of his life, Calvin never failed to point out when the opportunity arose that it

Martin Bucer's house at Strasbourg

would be better simply to use ordinary bread. However, he did not make an issue of this question, believing that there were more important points which demanded his attention.

To resume our narrative once more, at about this time, in the year 1539, Cardinal Sadoleto wrote a long letter, dated 18 March, to the syndics[3] and citizens of the town of Geneva. Using fine-sounding words, he sought to cajole them into turning away from Jesus Christ and he cast aspersions on the ministers whom God had used to bring about religious reform in the town. Sadoleto thought this was a good opportunity to inflict real harm on the cause of the gospel, since Calvin had been forced to leave the town the year before.

However, when news of these attacks reached Calvin some time later, he demonstrated his very real affection for the town of Geneva. In his concern for the well-being of the city, or rather for the defence of the truth of God against the accusations of this crafty fox, he replied with a long letter full of well-reasoned arguments. This letter, dated from Strasbourg on 1 September 1539, is included among his works in both French and Latin versions.

Calvin undertook at this time a revised and extended version of his *Institutes of the Christian Religion*, which was published on 1st August of that year. He also started writing on the letters of the apostle Paul, and dedicated his *Commentary on the Epistle to the Romans* to Simon Grynaeus, the foremost German scholar and his great friend. This commentary appeared in print on 18 October 1539.

Calvin also wrote a short, simple tract on the Lord's Supper in French, for the use of those who only spoke French. In this way, everyone could know what they should believe about the Lord's Supper and what benefits they should expect to receive in partaking of it. Even those whose understanding was very simple no longer had any reason to doubt. Five years later this book was translated into Latin, for the benefit of those who do not understand French. The translator, Nicolas des Gallars, was at the time a pastor at Geneva. He later went to London to help the French church in that city, and at the time of writing he is working in the church at Orleans.

It is worth noting the extreme care with which Calvin handles this subject, in this little book as well as in his *Institutes*. Having seen the unfortunate disputes which the question of the Lord's Supper had sparked off, to the point of causing splits within churches, he did all in his power to quench the fires of division with a clear exposition of the subject in which he did not take sides. He was singularly successful in this and anyone who examines his writings will see that, after God himself, it is Calvin whom we must thank for the solution to the problem which has since been adopted by all right-thinking people.

He also had the joy of bringing back to the faith very many of the Anabaptists who were being referred to him on all sides. Among these was a former abbot named Paul Volse, the man to whom Erasmus had dedicated his book *The Christian Knight* in 1518. After this man's conversion from Anabaptism, he became a minister of the church in Strasbourg, a post which he held until his death.

Another of Calvin's contacts was a man called Jean Stordeur, who was a native of Liège. Stordeur died in Strasbourg after contracting the plague. Some time later, on the advice of Pastor Bucer, Calvin married his widow, who was called Odilette, or Idelette, de Bure. She was a serious-minded woman of good character, and they lived together in peace and harmony until the Lord took her to be with himself. No child of this marriage survived infancy.[4]

In the year 1541, conferences were held in Germany at Worms and Ratisbon. These had been convened by the emperor in order to try to settle differences over matters of religion. Calvin was one of the first to be invited to attend on

the advice of the German theologians. His performance at these gatherings greatly enhanced his reputation, even among those who opposed him. Philip Melanchthon, for example, became a close friend from that time onwards, singling him out for the honour of being referred to as 'the theologian'.

Similarly, Gaspar Cruciger, a man of excellent qualities who was one of the pastors at the church in Wittenberg, took him to one side so that they could talk freely in private. In particular, he asked Calvin to explain to him in detail his understanding of the doctrine of the Lord's Supper. Calvin was very willing to comply. After their exchange of ideas, Cruciger, who was a good man and very human, thanked him heartily, stating that he saw things in the same light.

In Worms on New Year's Day, Calvin composed a poem in Latin, called a 'Song of Victory', in honour of Jesus Christ.[5] Attention has since been drawn to this work through the meddling of a prying monk from Toulouse, who condemned the song even before seeing it in print. Conrad Badius, who at the time of his death was minister of the church at Orleans, eventually translated it into French.

4.
Back to Geneva

While all these events were taking place the Lord was causing his judgements to fall on the town of Geneva. In particular he punished those who had held the post of syndic in 1538 and who were responsible for the expulsion of Farel and Calvin.

One of these men, who had been found guilty of insurrection, was killed as he tried to escape by jumping out of a window. Another was sentenced to be beheaded for a murder that he had committed. Finally, two former syndics were accused of fraudulent dealings in matters concerning the state. They fled the town and were found guilty in their absence.

Once the town had been cleared of such scum, people began to miss Calvin. Several delegations were sent to him from Geneva, and approaches were made to the leading citizens of Strasbourg through the good offices of their counterparts in Zurich. The men of Strasbourg raised objections to Calvin's proposed departure. He himself, seeing the fruits of his labours in this town, was equally reluctant to leave, notwithstanding the great affection in which he held the town of Geneva and the believers who lived there.

Once again it took threats of incurring God's judgement on himself by failing to obey this summons in order to convince him. It was Pastor Bucer who took this responsibility on himself, citing the example of Jonah. So, to the great regret of the leading citizens of Strasbourg, as well as that of Bucer himself and the other pastors, it was agreed that the town of Geneva should be allowed to have Calvin for a time.

All this took place before he was nominated to accompany Martin Bucer to the conference convened by the emperor at Ratisbon in 1541. Because of this he had to delay his return to Geneva.

The men in charge of the church in this city decided to request the leading citizens of Berne to allow M. Viret, who was then minister of the church at Lausanne, to come to Geneva for a time. This arrangement was to prevent the young church, which had already suffered so much, from disintegrating completely while awaiting Calvin's return.

Calvin was delighted to hear of this arrangement, knowing that it would be a great help to him to have Viret at his side when he returned. Several months later, after his return from Ratisbon, Calvin finally arrived in Geneva. The ordinary people, who now deeply regretted their earlier attitude towards him and were eager to hear their faithful pastor once more, welcomed him with such evident affection that it was soon decided that he would settle permanently in the town.

The authorities in Strasbourg agreed to allow Calvin to leave them on condition that he should remain a citizen of their town. They also wanted him to retain the income from a stipend that they had allocated to him by way of a salary for his lectures in theology. But Calvin was completely free from any desire to accumulate earthly possessions, and would not be persuaded to accept a single penny of this money.

So it was that on 13 September 1541 Calvin once again took up his former post in Geneva, where he was reunited with his friend and co-worker M. Viret. We can see in this God's wondrous mercy towards the people of this republic. Indeed, if the Israelites delayed their deliverance from Egypt by forty years by their rejection of Moses, we might have thought the

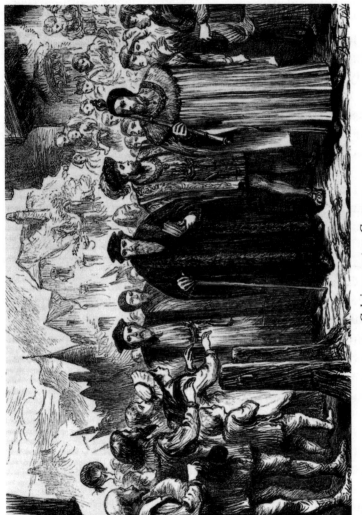

Calvin re-enters Geneva

people of Geneva deserved to remain permanently in bondage to Satan and the Roman antichrist for rejecting such faithful and worthy servants of the Lord as Calvin and his companions. However, God in his mercy allowed a delay of only three years in the building up of this church.

It is worth taking a little time to consider the manner in which Calvin took the situation in hand. From the outset, he only agreed to take on the responsibility of this church on the condition that a properly constituted consistory [i.e. a presbytery, or council of elders] should be set up and a workable system of church discipline drawn up. He considered such precautions to be essential and was anxious that they should be set in place as quickly as possible.

He therefore proceeded immediately, as instructed by the magistrates, to draw up the code of church discipline and practice which have remained unchanged ever since,[1] despite all the combined efforts of Satan and his followers to have them abolished, as we shall see in due course.

Calvin also promptly set about compiling the version of the catechism which is still in use today. He did not make any changes in doctrine from what was contained in the catechism which he had drawn up during his previous stay in Geneva, but this time he presented the material in the form of questions and answers to make it more easily understood by children. In the earlier work, the topics dealt with were simply summarized in short chapters.

This catechism can truly be classed as one of his finest works and one that has borne excellent fruit. It was so well received that it was translated from the original French into a number of other languages. Calvin himself translated it into Latin, dedicating the work to the ministers of the gospel in Eastern Friesland who had asked him if he would undertake such a task. Henri Etienne translated it into Greek, and Emmanuel Tremellius into Hebrew, since he was of Jewish nationality and taught theology at the University of Heidelberg. Both these men had a reputation as men of great scholarship and they were extremely proficient in these languages.

In time, the catechism came out in Italian, German, English, Gaelic, Flemish and Spanish.[2] The Latin, Greek and Hebrew versions are of value for use in schools as well as for winning Jews to Christ or for instructing Greeks.

Pierre Viret had only been loaned to the church in Geneva for a limited time. Calvin, who was by nature always inclined to look to the future and was anxious to secure for the church anything that he thought would promote its well-being, made numerous efforts to obtain agreement for his co-worker to remain permanently at his side.

With this objective in view, he wrote a number of letters to people whom he considered to be in a position to help. He himself attended a synod meeting in Vevey to make a formal request about this matter, but consideration for the church in Lausanne carried much weight in the final decision and prevented Calvin's request from being granted. However, it was agreed that Viret should stay on a few more months in Geneva, until things were more settled there. This was a great relief to Calvin, as he himself acknowledged.

Because of their close collaboration in these early days, Calvin continued afterwards to write frequently to Viret about the state of the church here. In these letters and in his correspondence with Farel he urged his colleagues to come and visit the church in Geneva as often as they could. For their part, both men have always demonstrated a remarkable degree of attachment to the church. They would hasten to the aid of their brother and fellow worker whenever their presence here would be of any help, which was very often the case.

The people too were delighted at the way these three worthy men got on so well together, and came willingly to hear them

preach. They remembered how in the early days the providence of God had brought these men together in the leadership
of the church.

Admittedly, there were still some who were ill-disposed
towards Calvin and found his presence in the city a source of
annoyance, especially when he was joined by the two others.
Such was the animosity of these men that they made fun of the
unity that existed between these three servants of God by
referring to them as 'the Tripod'. However, when all is said
and done, such godless people were either obliged to put a
good face on things or forced to admit that, in spite of their
opposition, God had united the hearts of the people with those
of his faithful pastors.

Shortly after his return to Geneva, in November to be exact,
Calvin learned of the death of Capito.[3] He grieved for a long
time over this news, seeing the passing of Capito as a great loss
to the church of God. Then, on top of that, came a rumour that
Bucer himself had been struck by the plague.

Calvin stayed in Geneva, the only one left of the three who
ought to have been there. He devoted himself to the government of the church and ensuring that nothing was neglected
that would contribute to the smooth running of its affairs.

There were other pastors in the town at that time. They
had been appointed after Calvin was driven out of the city,
and they remained after his return. Some of them did more
harm by their corrupt way of life than any good they did by
their teaching. However, knowing that it is always important
to try to avoid divisions in the church and to keep the peace as
far as possible, Calvin made an effort to spend some time with
these men. He admonished them as their spiritual state required, reproving them in private for their evil ways and
encouraging them to carry out their responsibilities out of
more than just a sense of duty. God eventually remedied the
situation by purging the church by various means of those who

were worthless. His judgement was clearly manifested where they were concerned.

Calvin, on the other hand, did not spare himself, working much harder than his health could stand. Every other week he would preach every day. He gave lectures in theology three times a week, and sat as a member of the consistory whenever it met to deal with cases of discipline. Every Friday, he would give a Bible Study at the meeting to discuss Scripture which we call the *'Congrégation'*. He was faithful in visiting the sick as well as those who needed personal help — not to mention the countless other matters that he had to deal with in the day-to-day exercise of his ministry.

In addition to all these tasks, he took great care of the believers in France, both by his letters to them, in which he instructed, exhorted, counselled and comforted them in the persecution they were suffering, and also by interceding on their behalf (or getting others to do so) whenever he thought he could see some means of doing so.

All this activity did not prevent him from continuing to work at his personal studies or from writing a number of very good and helpful books. In the next chapter we shall look at some of these works which were published in the early years of his ministry at Geneva. Then, in later chapters, we will introduce others in the course of the narrative.

5.
Calvin's writings up to 1549

Since the Sorbonne had for a long time been busy drawing up statements of faith whenever the fancy took them to do so, without basing them on any solid foundation, in 1543 Calvin wrote a very scholarly and well-reasoned book. In it he showed from the Word of God the true antidote to use against the false teachings and claims of these doctors of the church. The fact that these learned men failed to make any reply to this work is clear evidence of the superiority of Calvin's thinking over theirs.

In the same year, Calvin also drew up liturgical prayers for use in the church in Geneva, along with the forms to be used for the administration of the sacraments and the solemnization of marriages, as well as an exhortation for use when visiting the sick. All these writings are now included in the Psalter, together with a fine preface from the pen of their author, in which he discusses the use of singing in the public worship services of the church.

He also published a book, which he dedicated to Philip Melanchthon, in which he seeks to uphold the pure doctrine of Scripture against the claims of a man who was reputed to be one of the pope's greatest henchmen, namely Albert Pighius. Pighius argued strongly in favour of the free will of man.[1]

In 1544, Calvin wrote a short book called *On the Necessity for Reforming the Church*. He wrote it in the form of a plea

addressed to the Emperor Charles V on the occasion of his
meeting in the town of Spire with the princes and the authorities of states within the empire.

Pope Paul III had published an encyclical [i.e. a circular
letter addressed to all his bishops] in which he poured out his
venom against the emperor. In fact, Charles V, wanting to keep
the peace in Germany while he was engaged in a war with the
King of France, had decreed at the meeting in Spire that the
Protestants could be allowed to remain in the state and that
nothing should be attempted against them. He had also decided to convene a council at the earliest possible opportunity
to try to resolve the religious disputes.

Calvin therefore wrote certain comments *On the Fatherly
Admonition of Paul III to the Emperor*, in which he described
the great zeal manifested by the pope and showed that what the
latter was calling for was nothing but confusions contrary to
the Word of God. The pontiff, he said, seeks to destroy all
peace between men and despises the authority that God has
entrusted to civil rulers. At the same time, he leaves Rome to
its own devices and his own apostolic court wallows in all
kinds of evil excesses.

That same year, Calvin wrote two works in French, one
against the Anabaptists and the other against the Libertines.
These two books have since been translated into Latin by
Nicolas des Gallars.

In 1545, Calvin drew up a treatise on the manner in which
the believer is to conduct himself in his dealings with Roman
Catholics if he wants to avoid compromise with their superstitions.[2] To this he added a refutation of the arguments of
those who called themselves Nicodemites and also quoted the
views of Philip Melanchthon, Martin Bucer and Peter Martyr.
The following year he also published two sermons that he had
preached in Geneva on the same subject, and then, in 1549, the
notice addressed to the ministers at the church in Zurich on this
question. This book spoke to the hearts of many people in

France, who had previously been lulled to sleep in the midst of idolatrous practices. Calvin also translated his *Catechism* into Latin so that the churches who did not understand French would be able to have a taste of the form of doctrine which even young children were taught in Geneva.

In 1546 Calvin wrote his *Commentary on the two Epistles to the Corinthians* and took as the subject for his preaching the book of the prophet Isaiah.

He also published a short book in which he suggested that it would be most useful to draw up an inventory of all the relics alleged to exist by the papacy in France as well as Italy, Germany, Spain and elsewhere. In this work, the author is not content merely to expose the abuses and idolatry being committed, but also brings to light the flagrant lies told by priests when claims to possess a particular object were made in several different places at the same time. Calvin does not list every single instance of abuse, but he highlights enough examples to show that his allegations are well founded.

He originally intended to go on adding to his work as he received information from the various countries about further examples of abuse, which were without doubt much more widespread than is generally supposed. In fact, he would often tease his friends and family that they had not tried hard enough to find more examples of such things.

As far as France is concerned, however, there is, thank God, hardly anything left to fear in that quarter. The war has meant that so much of this trash has been taken away, seized or destroyed that it only remains for us to pray that God that will use means which cause less suffering for the people to do away with the little that remains. Nicolas des Gallars translated this book into Latin two years later.

1547 saw the publication of Calvin's book entitled The *Acts of the Synod of Trent, with an Antidote.* In it he deals in a most pertinent way with these revered church leaders and confirms the faithful in their belief in the simplicity of the doctrine taught in Holy Scripture. The quality of his book is such that these gentlemen who took part in the synod remained silent and were not able to put forward a defence of the decrees promulgated by their sessions. Their works were only of hay and stubble and were burnt up as soon as they were put to the test of the consuming fire of Holy Scripture.

Calvin also wrote his *Letter to the Faithful in Rouen.* In this he warned the believers not to be led astray by the errors of a certain monk, who was believed by some to be imprisoned for the sake of the Word of God, but who was really a Libertine who indulged in all kinds of wild and dangerous speculations.[3]

In 1548, Calvin wrote his *Commentaries on the Epistles of Paul to the Galatians, Ephesians, Philippians and Colossians*, as well as the *Commentary on the Two Epistles to Timothy*. He also published his book against the *Interim*[4] in which he shows that the only way to achieve real peace between Christians and an effective reform of the church is to keep to the Word of God, which is the doctrine of the prophets and apostles. It is no good, he says, trying to piece together a religion from various elements which are all the products of the human imagination. He also wrote against the laws of astrology to show that it was totally unfitting for Christians to indulge in such flights of fantasy. His reasoning leads him to draw judicious conclusions without wasting words in wearisome arguments.

So far I have listed only the works written by Calvin during the period between his return to Geneva and the year 1549. When we look at this list we cannot help wondering how he ever found the time to personally write, or at least dictate, all these works, in addition to carrying out all that is normally involved in the work of the ministry.

6.
Consolidating the work

Calvin's literary output, which we have just looked at, is all the more remarkable when we consider that he had a number of other grave causes for concern.

Leaving aside the question of his own illnesses, we should particularly note that he had to watch over his wife's health which was often failing in the years leading up to her death. He had the additional worry of the difficult pregnancy she went through and the serious illness that laid her low for several months in 1543.

At about the same time, Viret's wife was also struck by a long illness from which she eventually died. In 1546 Calvin himself suffered from an ulcer which caused him to have painful haemorrhoids. Farel and Viret were having to face serious problems in their own ministry and Calvin sought to take his share of the burden, showing his faithful companions the same brotherly care that they had manifested towards him.

At the same time, Calvin had his work cut out for him in seeing that discipline was maintained in some quarters. On several occasions the situation came close to degenerating into total chaos because of the malicious actions, or at least the double dealing, of those who should have been taking steps to put things right. This state of affairs was a great source of grief for Calvin.

Things got progressively worse up to the point where, on 16 December 1547, a disturbance, which threatened to turn into a riot, broke out actually during a session of the Council of Two Hundred. Calvin hurried to the council chamber as soon as he heard the news and was able to restore a degree of calm by appearing on the scene and interposing himself between the opposing factions.[1]

All these tensions threatened to distance him from his studies. However, he always took fresh courage in the Lord and hoped against hope that he would see something more positive and peaceful emerge as the fruit of all his labours in this church. God, in his mercy, finally granted that he should see such results in the last few years of his life here on earth.

In the meantime, Calvin was to face many serious difficulties in the years that followed,[2] but he overcame them one after the other, continuing in the work to which God had called him, and committing the results to him in simple faith.

Although, as the servant of the Lord, he was not answerable to men and did not measure success in terms of numbers — something which he had already amply proved — there is no doubt that God was pleased to sustain and encourage him through the growth of the church in Geneva. In fact, he was soon to see people of all ranks in life and from several different countries thronging to Geneva. Some came because they wanted to hear him on the quiet; others, by far the majority, came to join the church.[3] For this reason, the preaching was not just in French and Italian, as is still the case today, but also in English and Spanish.

The church grew to such an extent that the foreigners who came to settle in Geneva founded a society to meet the needs of those among their number who were poor, so that the responsibility for their welfare would not be borne by the town alone.

Old print of Geneva

That was not all. The French-speakers, realizing the great spiritual profit which could be reaped from the publication of Calvin's sermons, looked for a man with the skill necessary to set them down in writing. They employed him and paid him as adequate a salary as they could afford. God blessed this token of their affection so greatly that almost all of Calvin's sermons have since been written down and placed on record.

At this time there also began to be talk of making a collection of his lectures, transcribing them as he gave them. It is true that several people had already attempted this, both where the sermons and lectures were concerned. But so far no one had been able to take down the whole message, word for word. Up till then it had only been a question of noting down the main points and not of following all the thread of what he was saying. Nevertheless, Nicolas des Gallars, François Bourgoing and Jean Cousin, who were all three ministers of the gospel, are to be praised for undertaking these early attempts to record Calvin's preaching. Their work has paved the way for others to make further advances, and, if we may say so, to bring the work to perfection.

God bestowed outstanding gifts on Jean Budé, Charles de Jonviller and Denis Raguenier. The first two have kindly given us transcriptions of Calvin's lectures, while the third was employed by the *'Compagnie des Etrangers'* [the society founded to help the refugees] to record in writing the sermons of this worthy servant of God.

Because of this work, from now on I will mention in chronological order the books of the Bible expounded by Calvin in his lectures and sermons. In addition I will refer at appropriate points in the text to what he compiled in the way of commentaries as well as the topics treated in the congregational Bible Studies on Fridays. This list may appear long but in my opinion it is not superfluous, as it will give us a better understanding of how this good man gave himself unstintingly

Sketches of Calvin made by one of the students during his lectures

to the work. He was constantly busy cultivating the Lord's vineyard in a number of different ways at the same time — a fact which led Wolfgang Musculus,[4] a former minister of the church in Auspourg and later professor of theology at Berne, to describe Calvin, very aptly and in a good-humoured way, as 'a bow that was always tightly strung'.

But to return to the thread of our narrative, Calvin's wife died in March 1549.[5]

In May of the same year, he travelled to Zurich, accompanied by William Farel, in order to put in writing the agreement reached between the ministers, pastors and teachers of the church there and those in Neufchatel and Geneva. This agreement was concerned with the nature, value and purpose of the sacraments, the right use of them and the fruit to be expected from them.

As we have already seen, Calvin had already dealt with the subject of the Lord's Supper, and had done so in such a way that no one had any reason to take offence at what he said. Nevertheless, Satan did all he could to provoke a dispute in which Calvin would find himself in conflict even with this church in Zurich which he had always highly respected and honoured. However, the enemy strove in vain, for thanks to this meeting the servants of God remained in complete agreement, in harmony with all the churches of Switzerland and the region of Graubünden.[6]

A short time later, at the beginning of August to be exact, this agreement was printed in Latin and French. It has since been translated into other languages and has proved very helpful for the edification of believers everywhere.

On his return from Zurich, Calvin developed an inflammation of the shoulder which was very painful for a long time. However, he did not neglect any part of his ministry or the books that he had begun to write.

That year, on Sunday mornings he preached on the epistle to the Hebrews. Then, starting at the end of August, he continued with the Acts of the Apostles. On Sunday evenings, he preached on the Psalms, taking only those which had not yet been arranged in a metrical version (he had already preached on the others). He had reached Psalm 40. On the other days of the week, he preached on the prophet Jeremiah.

In his theological lectures, he expounded the book of the prophet Isaiah to students, ministers and other listeners. He had begun this study a long time previously. In addition, he devoted the congregational Bible Study on a Friday to the epistle to the Hebrews, and then to the so-called 'general' epistles. His writings for that same year comprised his commentaries on the epistle to Titus and the epistle to the Hebrews.

In August 1550 a prince, accompanied by a number of French noblemen, passed through Geneva on his way back from Rome. These men heard the whole of a sermon by Calvin on the text: 'They shall roar together like lions, they shall yell as lions' whelps' (Jeremiah 51:38). As usual, Calvin drew out the application of the text to the hearers in a manner that was marked by much grace, strength and simplicity and yet was completely lacking in ostentation. If all those present on that occasion had profited by what they heard, affairs in the kingdom [of France] would have run more smoothly and peacefully than they do. May God grant that even now they may think about these things before it is too late!

That year, having finished preaching on Jeremiah, Calvin continued in the ordinary weekday sermons with the Lamentations of the same prophet. After that, on 12 November, he embarked on a study of the prophet Micah. Meanwhile, in his lectures he expounded the book of Genesis, once he had finished going through the prophet Isaiah. At the congregational Bible Study on a Friday he expounded the Gospel of John.

He also had his *Commentary on the epistles to the Thessalonians* printed, as well as a book entitled *Concerning Scandals*. In this he showed that nothing should prevent us from embracing the gospel of Jesus Christ or from persevering in it to the end, as we have been called to do. He demonstrated that those who fall away do so because they do not truly know Christ.

Round about 1551, Calvin published the first edition of his *Commentary on Isaiah*. This work was carefully compiled from transcriptions of his lectures and sermons by M. des Gallars, who was then a minister of the church in Geneva. His *Commentary on the General Epistles*, as they are called, was also printed. For the sermons given during the course of the week, he preached that year on four Minor Prophets, beginning Zephaniah on 6 February, Hosea on 2 April, Joel on 5 September and Amos on 28 October.

That same year he was very distressed to learn the news of the death in England of his friend Bucer.[7]

7.
Under fire from Satan

At the point in time we have reached in our narrative, a formidable array of adversaries appeared on the scene and threatened the stability of the ongoing work. Of course, the enemies of truth had not waited until this moment to make their presence known, but it is at this time that we see the full might of the devil's artillery unleashed against the very foundations of the work that God was bringing to pass in Geneva.

Round about the year 1551, a man named Jerome Bolsec arrived in Geneva. He had at one time been a Carmelite friar in Paris, but had since exchanged the role of theologian for that of a doctor, or rather of a quack.

Under the impression that he was still shrouded in the darkness of the cloister, rather than in a church of God — of which he knew nothing except by hearsay — Bolsec began to draw attention to himself here and there, and even at meetings of the church, by saying evil things about the doctrines of God's providence and his eternal predestination.

Calvin immediately refuted his ideas, seeking to do so in a way that would put him back on the right track without giving him any grounds for bitterness or resentment. He restricted himself to replying publicly to Bolsec, so that those present at the meeting would not go away from the place having imbibed these false teachings. Calvin sought to put right what the former monk said rather than to attack him on a personal level.

The ministers of the church then summoned Bolsec to appear before them in private. This meeting took place on 15 May. They had a long talk with him and showed him from various passages of Scripture where he was at fault. However, he proved to be extremely obstinate, even though he did not put forward any valid arguments in defence of his position. He even went so far as to admit that he did not know how to explain a passage from Ezekiel to which the ministers drew his attention in order to show him that he was wrong.

After that, Bolsec refrained for a time from openly spreading his harmful teaching, but continued to do so in secret. However, since God was not willing to let him injure the flock, he once again brought his activities to light. This came about when, partly at the prompting of some people who were out to cause trouble, Bolsec began once more to voice his erroneous views openly in the meetings.

In the congregational Bible Study on Friday, 16 October, the passage expounded was John 8:47: 'He that is of God heareth God's words; ye therefore hear them not, because ye are not of God.' It was then that Bolsec launched into a long discourse, in which he said that we were making God the author of sin and blaming him for the condemnation of the wicked. According to Bolsec, we were making God out to be a tyrant or a 'Jupiter'. He added that we were trying to give the impression that Augustine was of the same opinion, when in fact neither he, nor any of the early church fathers, held this view. He ended by warning his hearers to take note of this new doctrine which many were teaching today, claiming that it had originated with Laurent Valla.[1]

Bolsec had the effrontery to believe that this was his chance to lead the people astray, as he did not think Calvin was present at this meeting. However, even if this had been the case, it is unthinkable that the other ministers present, not to mention William Farel, who had come from Neufchatel to visit the church and to see his friends, would have kept quiet. In any case, in the purposes of God, Calvin arrived incognito when Bolsec had just launched into his diatribe. He patiently waited for him to finish before coming forward and vigorously opposing this wolf in sheep's clothing. On the spot he answered point by point all the matters raised by Bolsec, speaking for the best part of an hour.

In his reply, Calvin not only presented much evidence from Scripture, but also quoted a great number of passages from the writings of Augustine, and showed himself to be so familiar with the latter that one would have thought that he had been reading and studying them that very day. In conclusion, in order to show up in its true light the impudent nonsense being put forward by Bolsec, he added, 'Would to God that the one who wanted to cite St Augustine in evidence here today had ever seen and profited from more of his works than the cover!'

After Calvin had finished speaking, Farel stood up and gave a further brief exhortation to the assembled congregation. Speaking with great earnestness and dignity, he urged that none of those present should turn away from the teaching of the Holy Scriptures.

The monk did not know what to say by way of reply. Among those present at the meeting was one of the officers of justice, who was very zealous for the truth. This man had Bolsec arrested as he left the church building and put in prison.

On more than one occasion over a period of several days, Calvin and his colleagues, responding to a summons from the officers of justice, spent a long time trying to convince Bolsec of his errors, both in writing and by the spoken word. The churches in other parts of Switzerland also gave their opinion, which agreed with that of Geneva, with the result that this enemy of the truth was left with no other refuge but an attitude of brazen monastic defiance, which he adopted when he appeared before the magistrates on 23 December. On this occasion, he was sentenced to banishment by a public proclamation, according to the usual custom.

No one should be surprised at the decision to banish him, for it has been obvious ever since, even with the situation as it is today, that he deserved such a fate. All right-thinking men will recognize this to be the case, seeing that he brought his judgement on himself, as the testimony of his own writings has proved repeatedly. This wretched man, who had deserved to be punished for stirring up trouble, was treated very leniently by the magistrate, because it was hoped that this action would cure him of his ignorant use of false reasoning.

He was subsequently guilty of causing many scandals and troubles in other churches in the area, and was expelled three times from the territory of Berne. After making himself a nuisance to everyone, he glorified God by publicly admitting he was at fault and, in particular, that he was troubled by a guilty conscience, at a meeting of the general synod of the French churches which was held at Orleans in 1562. After that, people began to have good hopes of him, but his evil nature soon reasserted itself and he has since reverted to the erroneous views he held at the beginning. He has been driven out from one place after another, as he deserves to be, and remains a living testimony, wherever he may roam, to the wrath of God revealed against those who resist the truth.[2]

As far as the upset he caused in the church in Geneva is concerned, there is no doubt that this would have led to serious trouble, had it not been for God's gracious provision of a remedy in the person of his servant. A number of the more gullible had let themselves be led astray, and those who were

out to cause trouble were delighted to be able to seize the
opportunity to start a fight. This incident showed the truth of
the apostle Paul's words when he said that it is when heresies
come that those who have followed the Word of God without
deceitfulness are revealed. Indeed, several of those who had
been led astray by this deceiver were restored to a better frame
of mind when the errors in his teaching were pointed out to
them.

There were some, however, who remained stubborn, in
particular a man who was well thought of and had made a good
impression in the world, and had even cut a good figure in the
church for some years. I am referring to Jacques de
Bourgogne, M. de Falais. He and his wife both at the same time
took the opportunity offered by this episode to turn away from
the doctrine held by our church, despite the fact that their
friends and servants, as well as the pastors, urged them to
revert to a better way of thinking.

As the December communion service was approaching, the
company of pastors decided that, as one of the means used to
bring all the membership into a holy unity of faith, they would
entrust to Calvin the responsibility of dealing with this whole
matter of predestination in the congregational Bible Study on
18 December. Afterwards, he and the other ministers from the
town and surrounding area would speak as they were led by
God to show how they were in complete agreement with this
article of faith. This was done, and not only the ministers but
several members of the laity, who were men of standing and
of considerable learning, also stated their beliefs, to the great
edification of all present. A formal record of the proceedings
of this *Congrégation* was printed in order to bear witness to
this solemn occasion.

Shortly afterwards — that is, at the beginning of 1552 —
Calvin's book on *The Predestination and Providence of God*
was printed, in which he proves the truth of this holy doctrine

in the best possible way. In this book he presents the beliefs of all the faithful churches, and in particular that of all the pastors of the church in Geneva, on this point, according to the teaching of the Scriptures. He also published the first volume of his *Commentary on the Acts of the Apostles*, which covers the first thirteen chapters of Acts.

For the ordinary sermons that year, Calvin began on 5 February to preach on Obadiah, and then went on to Jonah, Nahum and Daniel. On 21 November, he began the study of Ezekiel. Having completed his lectures on Genesis, he began an exposition of the Psalms.

Some time round about March 1553, Calvin set out, despite the bad conditions caused by rain and cold weather, to go to see William Farel, as he had heard that he was ill. This visit was a great comfort to Farel. He believed that he was nearing the end of his life and it was a joy to him to be able to talk once more with Calvin, his former companion in the Lord's work whom he had always admired and respected as one truly used by the Spirit of God.

After a stay of a few days, Calvin, seeing that the end was very near for his friend, decided there was no point in his staying any longer. He therefore left Farel apparently close to death, for, indeed, he was no longer able to speak. Even his doctor, Philibert Sarrazin, reckoned the end to be very near. However, against all hope, God soon afterwards restored Farel to health once more. His recovery disconcerted those ill-natured people who were, in their usual way, making fun of the situation and saying, 'The Tripod will have one foot missing now.'

That same year, Calvin dedicated his *Commentary on the Gospel according to St John* to the syndics and councillors of Geneva. He also began to expound his harmony of the three Gospels at the congregational Bible Studies on a Friday.

William Farel

It was at this time that Michael Servetus (who has already been mentioned in an earlier chapter) appeared on the scene. This Spaniard of cursed memory was not so much a man as a monstrous embodiment of all the heresies, old as well as new. He condemned the baptism of infants and, most serious of all, uttered atrocious blasphemies against the Trinity, particularly in relation to the eternal existence of the Son of God.

On his arrival in Geneva, Servetus was recognized by several who had already come across him elsewhere. He was arrested on 13 August on account of his blasphemies. With God's help Calvin argued so forcefully and with such intensity from the Word of God in refutation of his false teaching that Servetus was left with no defence other than his own indomitable obstinacy. Because of his unrepentant attitude, he was condemned on 27 October to be burnt at the stake as the righteous judgement of God and men on his crimes.

This put an end not only to his wretched life, but also to the blasphemies that he had been disseminating, both by the spoken word and in his writings, over a period of more than thirty years. No more need be said about this, seeing that Calvin specially wrote a book a short time afterwards — that is, in 1554 — in which he shows that a true faith rightly maintains that in the Godhead there are three persons who are of one substance. In this book he refutes the odious errors promulgated by the wretched Servetus, and proves that the authority of the magistrate extends to the suppression of heretics. He therefore maintains that it was with good reason that this wicked man, who showed such evident signs of being a reprobate, was put to death in Geneva.[3]

In 1554, beginning on 26 February, Calvin preached on the book of Job during the week. For the Sunday morning and evening services, having concluded the Acts of the Apostles, on 25 March he embarked on a study of the epistles to the Thessalonians. After that, on 16 September, he took as his subject the first epistle to Timothy. In January of the same year, he also published the second volume of his *Commentary on the Acts of the Apostles*, which covers from chapter 14 to the end of Acts. His *Commentary on the book of Genesis* came out in August.

One man, who was something of a dreamer and led a very disorderly life, had made false accusations in writing concerning the agreement over the sacraments which had been arrived at in 1549 between the churches of Zurich and Geneva. In response to these wild allegations, Calvin drew up a statement of the points covered by the agreement in question, and had this published in both Latin and French. On 28 November, he dedicated this statement to the pastors of the towns of Zurich, Berne, Basle, Schaffhausen, Chur and the areas coming under their jurisdiction, as well as those of all the regions of Graubünden, St Gallen, Bienne, Mulhouse and Neufchatel.

At the time when Calvin had to fight the teaching of Servetus, a very dangerous attack was brewing in the town and threatening the very existence of the church by denying it the authority to exercise discipline. In fact, some of the most eminent men, who held, or had usurped, power in the government of affairs, were not at all happy that the Word of God should be preached in sincerity and power. They were joined by a number of depraved persons who refused correction and whom the consistory had quite rightly forbidden to partake of the Lord's Supper until they gave evidence of repentance and changed their way of life. As I have said, these men had been plotting for a long time to disrupt the order of things, but up till now God had restrained them from exerting any significant influence.

These men could not, and indeed dared not, go as far as to abolish the consistory which exercised the spiritual jurisdiction that Jesus Christ had ordained for his church. But in their frustration with the state of affairs they went so far as to invoke the authority of the Council to grant absolution to those whom the consistory were preventing from taking part in the Lord's Supper and so allow them to receive the sacrament. To smooth the way for the adoption of this change, they proposed that one of the ministers should come to the Council, and that he should be present when the magistrates gave absolution to anyone who had been excommunicated by the consistory.

However, Calvin was so successful in exposing this conspiracy to the members of the consistory that it was decided that they would take the fight against their enemies into the Council chamber itself, acting in the name of the whole consistory. So Calvin and all the other ministers, both from the town itself and from the neighbouring villages, went in person to complain to the leaders of the Council about those of their number who were plotting such things (without, however, mentioning any names). The pastors stated firmly that not one of them would agree to be party to such a corrupt practice, but that if the change went ahead they would be forced to give up their ministry in the church in Geneva.

Now, in spite of the opposition of the consistory and all the pastors, a man called Ami Perrin, who was at the time the leading syndic (and of whom we shall hear more), decided to take action. He gave a man of bad character whom he favoured[4] a letter authorizing him to receive communion when in fact he had been excluded from taking part in it. Perrin and his party evidently imagined, either that Calvin and the other ministers would not dare to refuse to allow him to take part when he attempted to do so in the presence of the gathered congregation, or else that their refusal would provoke an outcry that would be particularly damaging to the pastors. But God was to show that the grace he gives his servants to stand firm has a much more solid foundation than the obstinacy of the wicked.

Although Calvin had only learnt of the conspiracy two days before the first Sunday in September, which was the date of the next communion service, he made up his mind to do his duty at all costs. His fellow-workers all supported him in this resolve. They did not allow fear of reprisals to cause them to profane the holy sacrament by administering it to a trouble-maker, who wanted to destroy the framework of church order which had long been established in this church and helped preserve its sanctity.

Towards the end of his sermon on the Sunday in question, Calvin exhorted the church to partake of the Lord's Supper with all due reverence. He then went on to state that he would rather die on the spot than allow those who had been excluded from the Lord's Table to take part. If any of them tried to do so, in spite of his warning, he added, they would know what to expect. These words took the troublemakers by surprise and they did not dare to come forward for the communion.

In the course of the afternoon service that day, Calvin took as his text the passage in chapter 20 of the Acts of the Apostles, in which the apostle Paul addresses the elders of the church at Ephesus. He gave a fine word of exhortation to the whole church on the apostle's words, when he said, 'Therefore watch, and remember, that by the space of three years I ceased not to warn everyone night and day with tears. And now, brethren, I commend you to God and to the word of his grace...' (Acts 20:31-32). The preacher stated that he was always ready to serve the whole church, both in private and in public. However, in view of the current state of affairs, he did not know whether this might prove to be the last time he preached in Geneva. Indeed, those who held power in the town were trying to force him to act in a way which God had forbidden. He therefore encouraged the people to look beyond the person of the preacher and to hold firmly to the Word of God that had been preached to them. 'I must therefore speak to you', he said, 'in the same way as did the apostle Paul and say, "Brethren, I commend you to God and to the word of his grace."'

Calvin preaching in the Cathédrale St Pierre

The subject continued to occupy the Council for about a year before the proposal was finally dropped. However, God honoured the firm stand taken by his servants and it was eventually decided, after consultation with the Swiss churches, that the consistory would remain in its existing state, without losing any of the authority to adjudicate in spiritual matters that it had previously been entitled to exercise.

8.
The sword and the trowel

When they saw that they had failed to bring down the authority of the consistory, in 1555 the party of troublemakers, led by Perrin and his accomplices, prepared to resort to violent means in an attempt to attain their objective. They used as a pretext the arrival of a number of French people who had come to settle in the town. The objectors, who were some of the leading men of the city, claimed that they were afraid of treachery on the part of the newcomers.

Perrin and his associates wanted to be rid not only of many of the French, but also of the upright men whose presence in the government was proving prejudicial to their plans. This would have allowed them to make whatever changes they wanted to the state of affairs, both in the town and in the church.

But, in the will of God, they themselves gave away their conspiracy one evening through the careless talk of some of their number who had been drinking. As a result their leaders found themselves in a very awkward position, and all they could do was to make a quick getaway, forfeiting their honour in the process and suspecting that their lives were at stake.

God alone knows whether Calvin, who was the prime target of the conspiracy, was ever tempted to slacken in the fearless execution of his duty by the thought of the dangers he incurred, either before or after the plot was discovered. What is certain is that the exposure of this conspiracy contributed greatly to the advancement of the church of God. Indeed, as a result the people became more obedient to the Word of God, the sacred task of reforming the church was carried on more effectively, and any scandals were duly punished and suppressed. Calvin rejoiced in the Lord over this state of affairs. In fact, it was plain to see that the joy he felt at the improvement in the situation was also beneficial to his health and inspired him with renewed energy and zeal in his service to the church.

It is true that this conspiracy generated an inordinate amount of work and exposed him to countless dangers, but in the end, the Lord, in his great mercy and through the wisdom given to his servant, brought the matter to the conclusion which has already been described — that is, to a state of tranquillity and happiness far in excess of anything this city had ever known.

On 20 March of that year, Calvin began to preach on the book of Deuteronomy in the ordinary weekday services. On 21 April, following on from his exposition of Titus, he took as the topic for his Sunday sermons the second epistle to Timothy. Then, on 20 October, he turned to 1 Corinthians.

Calvin also had his *Harmony of the three Synoptic Gospels* printed, in which he shows how well the evangelists agree with each other. Finally, he took the book of Psalms as the topic for the congregational Bible Study each Friday.

At this time, attention was focused on a local lawyer called Matthew Gribaldi, the lord of Farges, who held to the false teaching of Servetus and was secretly disseminating it in various places. When this man visited Geneva, he was summoned to appear before the company of pastors, who were joined by certain members of the Council and elders from the consistory. This meeting was held so that they could confer with Gribaldi and seek to put him right.

The lawyer arrived accompanied by a number of Italians. (I believe he had at one time lived in Italy and had taught law in the town of Padua.) When he came in, he asked in Latin, 'Where is Calvin?', holding out his hand as if to offer it to Calvin.

Calvin answered, 'Here I am', but did not go on to take his hand because, as he said, 'It does not make sense for me to shake hands with you until we can agree about doctrine. We must not begin with formalities.' At that, Gribaldi promptly left saying, 'Farewell, gentlemen.'

He was then called to the town hall to explain to the members of the Council the reasons for his refusal to discuss doctrine with the assembled ministers. He complained on this occasion that when he had gone to Calvin's home, the latter had refused to talk to him. He added with a show of bravado: 'I have already talked to princes, kings and emperors.'

To this Calvin replied, 'M. de Farges boasts of having talked with princes and kings, whereas I refused to speak to him. Speaking for myself, I do not boast of having talked to great noblemen. I will simply say that every day I talk to all those who need to see me, even the youngest and the poorest. As far as M. de Farges is concerned — a man whose own writings testify that he upholds errors which are contrary to the most important tenets of our faith, I did not want to become involved in a debate with him without any witnesses being present. That would have been a waste of time. I know what people of this sort are like. He, on the other hand, refused to hold discussions with me in the presence of a large gathering.'

Calvin then went on to refute the errors taught by Gribaldi, who left Geneva soon afterwards. The renowned Duke of Württemberg expelled him from the University of Tübingen for the same reason. As he continued to utter blasphemies he was imprisoned by the authorities in Berne, but was later released on the grounds that he had renounced his beliefs as heretical. He remained in the region of Berne until September 1564, when he died of the plague, without having changed his views.[1]

In May 1556 Calvin suffered from a fever. At first he paid no attention to the symptoms of this illness. His fellow-workers wanted to arrange for someone to take over the preaching, to relieve him of this burden, but he did not think this necessary. He suffered a second attack of the fever on Sunday, 10 May. During the service that day, Calvin was due to preside at the induction of two new pastors, one as a replacement for a pastor who had died and the other in place of a man who had been deprived of office for embezzlement.

Calvin took no notice of his fever, or chose to ignore it (he took such great delight in serving the church). Shortly before he left his house to go to church, it could be seen from the trembling of his fingers that the illness was coming on, but he concealed this and went up into the pulpit. After the opening prayer and the singing of a psalm, he began to preach and made a great effort to carry on even though he was ill. He had a chair brought up into the pulpit so that he could sit down. However, as he continued to be racked by fits of shivering, he was eventually forced to make his excuses to the congregation and go home without having finished his sermon. To make up for his

Calvin's chair in the pulpit of the Cathédrale St Pierre, Geneva

absence and so that the induction service should be brought to a fitting conclusion, one of the other ministers present, Nicolas des Gallars, completed the sermon, skilfully taking up and continuing the exposition of the text that Calvin had begun.

On 16 July of that year, Calvin took as his subject for the ordinary weekday services the book of the prophet Isaiah, which he had already preached on in the church and at the college.

On 26 August, accompanied by several friends, he left for Frankfurt at the request of the leading men of that town. They had in fact asked him to come to settle some problems that were troubling the French church which had been established in the town through the kind offices of the authorities there. Much to the satisfaction of the nobles of Frankfurt, his trip was a complete success and was a great help to the church there.

On his return from this trip, the pressures of work combined with the effects of the long journey to trigger an attack of haemorrhoids and he also suffered a recurrence of his old problem with an ulcer. However, he did not take to his bed, or neglect any of his duties.

That year Calvin penned a short book which he called *Reforms to silence a certain knave.*[2] He wrote this work as a result of the arrival in Geneva of this man, accompanied by a prostitute who was his mistress. The man's true character came to light, as that of a shameless deceiver, and he was forced to leave. So he withdrew to Lausanne, and then to the area around Berne, and generally behaved in such a way that he was banished on pain of flogging.

He was so vexed by this that on his return to France he had a letter printed which he addressed to 'Their excellencies the syndics of Geneva'. In this letter, he made disparaging remarks about Calvin's doctrine and also that of the church and of the college at Lausanne. This letter did not go unanswered, thank God, and the reply was enough to satisfy (or rather to annoy) this man so that he has kept quiet ever since. He does not seem to have had anything worthwhile to say.

In addition to all this, in the same year, Calvin set about revising his commentaries on all of Paul's epistles, as well as that of the epistle to the Hebrews and the general epistles. While he was doing so, he dedicated the *Commentary on the First Epistle to the Corinthians* to the nobleman Galeazzo Carraciolo, Marquis of Vico. This replaced his earlier dedication of the work to M. de Falais, who had rebelled and adopted the heretical views of Jerome Bolsec.

9.
Keeping up the good fight

In 1557 Calvin published his *Commentary on the Psalms* and had his *Lectures on the prophet Hosea* printed. He also wrote three replies, or 'admonitions', in Latin addressed to a man called Joachim Westphal, who was trying to undermine the sound doctrine relating to the Lord's Supper. Calvin declared in the third of these papers that if this man did not return to the truth then he would consider that he was deliberately being obstinate. However, Westphal continued to stick rigidly to his position, so that eventually in 1558 I myself took up my pen to answer him and refuted all his arguments.

On the last day of February, Calvin began preaching on the second epistle to the Corinthians in his Sunday sermons. After that, he took the epistle to the Galatians, beginning on 14 November. On 15 May 1558, he began expounding the epistle to the Ephesians on Sundays.

As for his writings, in addition to those composed while he was suffering from ague (which I will mention later), at the beginning of the year he penned a *Reply to the slanders of a certain dreamer*. This man, without revealing his identity (it was in fact Sebastian Castellio), was trying to bring the holy doctrine of God's secret providence into disrepute. I too have replied at length to this man's false accusations.

Since Castellio gave the appearance of being all sweetness and light while trying to make Calvin out to be a very harsh and bitter man, it will be helpful if I say a little more about him, so that everyone will be able to see what kind of man — or, perhaps I should say, what a monster — this Sebastian Castellio really was. Calvin made it quite clear that he would have been happy to leave Castellio in peace if the latter had not forced a confrontation on him by misrepresenting sound doctrine.

Because of his knowledge of languages and, in particular, his proficiency in Latin, Castellio was appointed as principal of the college in Geneva. Being by nature prone to egotism, he gave himself up so completely to his vanity that in the end he was wholly swallowed up by it. He could not be persuaded to take the trouble to read commentaries or other writings to make him change his mind.

He openly condemned one of the books that forms part of the canon of Scripture saying that it was dirty and indecent. He was referring to the Song of Songs, a book which sets forth a wonderful mystery, using language and pictures drawn from everyday life, as the early church fathers, in particular Gregory and Bernard, have clearly demonstrated.

After being given a reprimand, Castellio publicly launched into hurling abuse at the pastors of the church in Geneva. The magistrates ordered him to substantiate his allegations, and when he could not do so, dismissed them as malicious slanders. He was ordered to make a public confession of his guilt and then to leave the town.

He withdrew to Basle and caused no more trouble until the affair blew up of Jerome Bolsec's attack on the doctrine of predestination. Castellio, who had always secretly and in private held the Anabaptist view on perfection, but who was prepared to come to terms with all and sundry, now came out into the open over this issue. He was also very annoyed about the death of Servetus.

Using the pen name of Martin Bellie, he began by publishing a book which he had printed in both Latin and French. I have personally written a reply to the errors and blasphemous statements contained in this work.

Writing under the name of Theophilus, he followed this with a treatise called *Theologica Germanica* in Latin and *Traité du vieil et nouvel homme [Treatise Concerning the Old and New Man]* in French. Finally, he produced versions, or rather distortions, of the whole Bible in Latin and French, in which he displayed such an odd combination of presumption and ignorance that, were it not for the fact that novelty always attracts those of an ambitious turn of mind — of whom we have seen more than ever in the present century — one might wonder what any intelligent person could see of interest in his writings.

In order to illustrate the mistakes made by Castellio in his French translation of the Bible, as a result of his stubbornness and refusal to take good advice, I quote here what Calvin had to say on the subject in a letter to one of his friends, written in 1542:

Let me tell you about the comical way M. Sebastian is behaving, which will both sadden and amuse you at the same time. The other day he came to ask me if I could not see what a good idea it would be to publish his translation of the New Testament.

I replied that it was badly in need of correcting in a number of places. He asked me why. I showed him, from the three or four chapters that he had submitted for me to look at a long time ago. He assured me that he had been more careful in his work on the rest.

However, to give you an idea of his level of ability and of faithfulness to the original text, I will cite an example. He goes to so much trouble to change ordinary words that he ends up by altering the meaning of the passage. Where the text says, 'The Spirit of God dwells

in us', he puts, 'who haunts us'. Now 'to haunt' means 'to
frequent', or 'to come from time to time', and not 'to
dwell'. Even one little error like this, in something so
elementary, is enough to discredit the whole translation.
As far as I am concerned, I do not want to waste my time
lingering over such trifles.

To return to what we were saying earlier, when Castellio
had his Latin translation of the Bible printed in Basle, he
prefaced it with a letter addressed to the late good King
Edward of England. In this preface, on the pretext of preaching
love to others, he undermines the authority of the Scriptures,
calling them obscure and imperfect. He refers us instead to
private revelations — in other words, to the dreams of
whoever first happens to come along.

He also included certain comments on the ninth chapter of
the epistle to the Romans, in which he is clearly teaching
Pelagianism.[1] He refuses to recognize anything which is not in
itself good as having been decreed by God. He thus invents the
idea of God permitting that which is contrary to his will and
accuses us of making God out to be the author of sin.

None of this affected the faithful servant whom God had
placed in Geneva, especially since all these errors and false
accusations had already been dealt with time and time again.
However, the opposition put together a collection, in Latin, of
certain articles of faith and arguments which some people
claimed had been taken from the writings of Mr John Calvin,
and supplied answers to them. This booklet was sent by special
courier to Paris to be printed there. But God was watching over
all that was happening and caused the original manuscript to
fall into our hands. We have since had it printed ourselves,
together with the answers it deserves.

When Castellio got wind of this, he did not know what
answer to give to the pastors and ministers of Basle. He

contented himself with denying that he was the author of these articles. Soon afterwards he was summoned to appear in Basle, where a debate was in session, in order to explain his beliefs on the subjects of free will and the providence of God, and his doctrine was condemned.

As, some years earlier, he had been appointed professor of Greek by those who were not aware of his heretical views, he was ordered not to meddle with anything in future, either in speech or in writing, but to confine himself strictly to his work as a teacher. He promised to do this, but he could not bring himself to adhere totally to these conditions, as he continued spreading his delusions whenever the opportunity arose.

At a time when, to my great regret, I found myself unable to leave France because of the civil wars, Castellio, who was motivated by, at the very least, an inordinate ambition and by the hatred that he felt towards me, wrote a booklet entitled *Advice to France in Distress*. He did not put his name to it, or mention the place where it was printed, although he was living in a free town. In this booklet, he accuses all the French churches of rebellion and insurrection. He advises everyone to follow his own opinions, thus opening the door to every form of heresy and false doctrine.

I did not deign to reply to this 'advice', which revealed far too much of the author's ponderous style, his ignorance of his subject matter and his lack of experience in such things. Instead, I replied to several charges he had made against me, interspersing his accusations with unspeakable errors that could not be allowed to pass unchallenged, under the pretext of defending the points I had attacked in his Latin translation.

This reply of mine, which was dedicated to the pastors of the church in Basle, led to Castellio's being summoned to appear before that church, and then before the leading men of the town. He was ordered to reply to my accusations, which I offered to prove from his own writings. However, he was saved the trouble of complying by his death which occurred shortly after these events.

No doubt some will deplore the amount of space I have devoted to this subject, thinking that my words are those of an angry man who cannot even bear to let the dead rest in their graves in peace.[2] But God knows that I never hated the man when he was alive, and that I never had any dealings with him in private, either for good or ill, that might now cause me to hate or to want to harry the dead whom it is for the Lord to judge. However, it was necessary to refer to all this to put people on their guard against the writings and the followers that this man has left behind.

That same year, among the many prosperous people who belonged to the Italian church in Geneva, most of whom were God-fearing, faithful believers, there were certain individuals who began, secretly and as the opportunity arose, to revive some of the heresies taught by that scoundrel Servetus. They disseminated blasphemies against the three persons of the Godhead, depriving Christ of his divinity, sometimes openly but often in a roundabout manner. One of these people was a man from Calabria called Valentin Gentile. There was also a man of Sardinian nationality and Jean-Paul Alciati, who was from Piedmont, as well as a doctor named George Blandrata who was originally from Saluzzo.

When the pastor of the Italian church discovered that some of his congregation were secretly entertaining this poisonous teaching, he consulted Calvin. On the latter's advice, a confession of faith on the subject was drawn up, which everyone would be expected to sign after the leadership had brought it before the congregation. Those who had any difficulty with the statement of faith would first be given an opportunity to express their reservations and to have these points explained to them.

This meeting took place on 18 May, in the presence of the pastor, the elders and all the membership of the Italian church, as well as Calvin and the other Genevan ministers. Several prominent citizens, who had been deputed to attend by a resolution of the Council, were also present.

In the course of this gathering, a number of people stood up and voiced their opposition to the best of their ability for a period of three hours — in particular this man Jean-Paul Alciati, whom I have already mentioned by name. But, by the grace of God, Calvin answered all the objections so well and explained these matters so clearly that all the members of the Italian church signed the confession in question, with the exception of six people, one of whom was Valentin Gentile. These men were later summoned to a private meeting and then gave their approval to the document.

Now this Valentin afterwards continued secretly to spread his poisonous doctrine. Wherever he went he would let fall some remarks about his erroneous beliefs in order to lead simple souls astray and attract others to his way of thinking. When his behaviour was discovered, the city officials summoned him to appear before them and his failure to keep his word was brought to light.

Finding no way of escape, he claimed that he had continued to talk about these things because his conscience would not let him keep silent. He maintained this at such length and to such good effect that he was granted another hearing on these points, in the presence of a good number of learned men of great renown. Calvin plied Gentile with so many arguments from Scripture that the latter did not know what to say, except that he did not understand anything about the art of conducting a public debate.

He afterwards put his views down on paper and sent them to the important men of the town. He also submitted his opinion in writing to three ministers of the church in Geneva, quoting several passages from the writings of the early church fathers in his own support.

But Calvin replied to this, also in writing, the very next day, showing beyond any question of doubt that Gentile was shamelessly distorting what the church fathers had said. Finally, fearing that he would suffer the same fate as Servetus, Valentin Gentile agreed to fall into line, declaring that he now accepted the truth and realized that he had been in the wrong. He wrote a lengthy statement testifying to his repentance.

Although some considered this volte-face on his part not to be genuine, it meant that the sentence passed against him was limited to his being led, to the accompaniment of blasts on a horn, to each of the crossroads in the town, where he was to beg for pardon, with his head uncovered, clad only in a shirt and carrying a lighted torch. He was required to publicly burn his writings, which he did meekly enough.

He was also forbidden to leave the town without first obtaining permission to do so. He had to stay in prison until he raised a sum of money to put down as bail. These measures were intended to stop him from going elsewhere to disseminate his heretical teaching and to confirm that his repentance was genuine. But on 5 September of the following year, he submitted a formal request to the authorities asking to be freed from the terms of his bail. He claimed that he did not have the means to raise the money because of his status as a foreigner. They had therefore to be content with his promise, which he immediately broke by secretly fleeing the city to go and take refuge with that visionary Matthew Gribaldi, who has been mentioned earlier.

As for George Blandrata, he had often held private conversations with Calvin about the doubts that he still entertained relating to the question of the Trinity. Each time, Calvin would answer him and explain everything to him very clearly, with the result that Blandrata would say he was satisfied. However, some time later, he would begin once more to express the same doubts, in the way that those who do not know how to accept what the Word of God teaches are carried away by their own fantasies and are slaves to their own pride and stubbornness.

Seeing what was happening, Calvin told Blandrata at their last meeting, in the presence of witnesses, that it would be best if they put down in writing a summary of their conversation and the areas where they were in agreement, so that they would not have to keep on going over the same ground. This was done, and Blandrata put his signature to the points listed.

However, not long afterwards, when he was present at one of Calvin's lectures, Blandrata saw a bailiff (or, as we would say in Geneva, a watchman) come in. The man was waiting for one of the syndics who was attending the lecture. At the sight of him (such is the effect of a guilty conscience, which trembles at the mere rustle of a leaf), Blandrata imagined that someone was coming to arrest him. He immediately fled the town, although no one was pursuing him.

Eventually, these three accomplices met up again in Poland, where they continue to this day to stir up endless trouble. As we shall see in a later chapter, Calvin's writings have helped greatly to build up the Polish churches, strengthening those who are faithful and rendering the enemies of the truth powerless. We may therefore hope that these troublemakers will not be slow to feel and recognize the power of this servant of God, and that with God's help their downfall may be imminent.

10.
Treasure in earthen vessels

In 1558, at the time of the grape-harvest, Melchior Volmar, that worthy German whom Calvin had known in his youth at Bourges, came to Geneva especially to see him. Volmar had been wanting to make this trip for a long time, as much for the sake of the friendship he felt for Calvin as that of seeing for himself the great blessing that God had poured out upon Calvin's labours in terms of the growth of the church in Geneva.

Around the month of September, God's servant suffered a long and painful attack of ague, during which he was forced to give up preaching and teaching. However, he continued to work at home, even though people told him he should not and urged him to take more care of himself.

So it was that, in addition to the many letters that he wrote to various people and the advice that he gave by word of mouth on a number of topics, he began putting the finishing touches to his final version of the *Institutes*, in both the Latin and French editions.

While the preface to this work was being printed, news reached Calvin from Augsburg, the seat of the imperial government, that reports were rife that he had revolted against the papacy and that these were causing quite a stir. The princes and their courts had been too credulous in accepting the truth of this rumour.

However, these reports failed to discourage Calvin from faithfully continuing to carry out the work to which he had been called. In fact, it was at this very time that he undertook the complete revision of his commentary on Isaiah, which he had already had printed in 1551 but which he now had completely reset.[1]

He also had his *Lectures on all the Minor Prophets* printed. Up till then only those on the prophet Hosea had been published. He was taken ill with the fever just at the time when he was about to complete this series of lectures. He had only two or three studies on Malachi still to give. So, in order not to delay the publication of the work any further, when the printer reached this point in the typesetting, Calvin gave these remaining lectures to a small group of listeners assembled in his bedroom (since his fever and the cold winter weather prevented him from leaving the house).

His illness lasted for some eight months and was so severe that it laid him low during that time. Even on the evenings when the fever left him, he could not eat anything until the evening of the following day, so that he often went for up to forty-eight hours without eating or drinking. But that meant that all night long his throat would feel very dry. His long years of adopting a very frugal and abstemious lifestyle, and of keeping a tight rein on all his appetites, helped him to endure this incredibly painful trial. Sometimes the doctors argued with him, telling him that he was not taking enough liquid. He would then force himself to take a little soup in the evening when the fever subsided. But some hours afterwards he would have an attack of migraine which caused him almost as much suffering as the fever itself. So he had to revert to going without food or drink for long periods of time.

At about this time — that is, in March 1559 — M. Pierre Viret and a number of others found themselves obliged for good reasons to leave the place where they were living and came to settle in Geneva. The city magistrates joined Calvin and the other ministers in urging Viret to take over pastoral responsibility for the church to fill the gap created by Calvin's long absence due to his illness.

It was in this same month of March 1559 that, in the will of God, the invalid was at last quit of his fever. However, it had so seriously undermined his health that he never fully recovered. From then onwards, he had a limp in his right leg, which was very painful at times. For all that, he would not give up and stay at home, except on a few occasions when he was racked with pains far too severe for him to ignore.

He therefore continued to go to the church to preach and to the lecture-hall to give his lectures. Sometimes he would walk there by himself, but at other times he would lean on someone's arm for support. When he was incapable of doing anything else, he would arrange to be carried in a chair or would ride a horse.

His first return to the pulpit following his illness was an occasion of great joy for the whole church. I remember that it was a Sunday and that we were singing Psalm 30, which was a wonderful opportunity to give thanks to God for his servant's recovery. You could see from Calvin's face how he thanked God for this blessing, with a true sense of reverence and artless devotion, completely devoid of any affectation (something which he is known to have always shunned).

Having thus resumed the exercise of his duties, he concluded his exposition of the remaining chapters of Isaiah during the ordinary weekday sermons. Then, on 4 September, he began preaching once more on the book of Genesis. In his lectures, he began the prophet Daniel on 12 June. From July onwards, he began preaching on a Sunday on the harmony of the three Synoptic Gospels. There are sixty-five of these sermons in print.

Towards the end of December, he began to spit blood as the result of an illness which was gnawing away at his lungs and which had been brought on by overwork. He was in fact not allowing himself any rest at all and was still continuing to carry out all the many duties for which he was responsible.

This problem could well have given him serious cause for alarm, but after taking treatment advised by his doctors and having just a few days' rest, he went on in his usual way and began preaching once more. His doctors and close friends, however, advised him to rest for at least a month in the hope of curing the disease while it was still in its early stages.

In fact, the lack of rest to which he continued to subject his delicate constitution led to two or three relapses in the course of the next few years. On these occasions, the doctors again helped him to the best of their ability, given that they found themselves dealing with a body that was so badly worn out.

I should not omit to mention at this point the great joy that God granted him when he prompted the magistrates and governors of the town to follow Calvin's advice and take the courageous step of laying the foundations of a school for the teaching of the principal languages. Several excellent men who had come to Geneva with M. Pierre Viret were employed as teachers in this school.

This school first saw the light of day at a time when, as everyone knows, this town was facing very grave threats on account of the gospel, and it seemed that it would not be possible to go on with the Reformation for much longer.[2] Calvin knew what it meant to depend on God and taught the same lesson to others in respect to every area of life.

Some time round about the end of the year 1559, the congregational Bible Study on a Friday began the exposition of the last four books of Moses in the form of a harmony, following the approach adopted by Calvin in the commentary that he has since had printed. In April 1560 he concluded his lectures on the prophet Daniel and around the middle of the month he began lecturing on Jeremiah.

In June, the brethren in Poland warned him about the trouble being caused in their churches by a man called Stancarus, who claimed that Jesus Christ was only our mediator in his human nature, and not in regard to his deity.[3] The brethren sent Calvin a summary of Stancarus' arguments and asked him to reply to these points. He dealt with them briefly, but very forcefully, in a letter addressed to the churches in Poland. He has since composed a second reply on this subject, at the request of the Polish believers, in order to stop Stancarus spreading his fanciful and harmful speculations.

Still in the year 1560, Calvin set about revising his commentaries on the Acts of the Apostles, making additions in a number of places. He also learnt of the death of M. Philip Melanchthon, who had written to him some time previously expressing his wish to come to Geneva to see him and to find solace in his company.

In 1561, a messenger brought letters from the King of France to the syndics and Council of the town of Geneva. In these letters, the king stated that he had been informed that the troubles affecting his kingdom originated with the people of Geneva and the ministers there. Calvin and his companions were requested to appear before the Council to answer these accusations.

Calvin showed in this affair that he served God without sparing himself, for, he replied, far from stirring up the confusion reigning in the kingdom of France, he had done all he possibly could to prevent it. He was ready, if the king so wished, to appear before him personally to clear his name on this and all other matters raised, and to answer all the charges against him, so confident was he that his conscience was clear.

The Genevan authorities accordingly replied to the king in these terms. Such a step could not be taken without putting Calvin's life in danger, for it is well known how unrelenting was the hostility towards him of the pope's followers in France, of all ranks of life. As for Calvin himself, he was not concerned for his own life, but only for the advancement of the kingdom of Jesus Christ.

On Friday, 3 February of that same year, he began preaching on the book of Judges during the week. On Friday, 8 August, he went on to the books of Samuel. As for his writings, he replied to the slander of a man called Tileman Hesshusius, who had written at length criticizing Calvin and seeking to undermine the pure doctrine concerning the Lord's Supper.

This man Tileman Hesshusius had become so irate on the subject of the Lord's Supper that on an earlier occasion Philip Melanchthon had been obliged to characterize him as particularly stubborn in his reply to the Count Palatine Frederick, who wanted to know Hesshusius' views on the Lord's Supper. Melanchthon's reply has since been printed in Heidelberg.

Among other things that happened in that same year, 1561, Valentin Gentile (who has been mentioned earlier), or someone else writing under his name, had a short booklet printed in Lyons. This pamphlet, which was in Latin, contained a number of heretical propositions and blasphemies against the holy Trinity. Calvin published a reply to it and at the same time made public the action which had been taken against Valentin Gentile in Geneva, not only in the Italian church but also his appearance before the leading men of the town which took place actually within the prison where he was confined. Calvin showed how Gentile, after having made a public declaration that he renounced his errors, had nevertheless later reverted to his original position and was guilty of vile blasphemy and of breaking his word.

Calvin's lectures on Daniel were also printed at this time. He dedicated them to all the believers in France who longed to see the advancement of Christ's kingdom in that land. One might say that he showed himself to be a true prophet in the letter of dedication that he addressed to them. In fact, at that time it seemed that the true church in France could hope to experience a measure of peace, and that there would be great liberty for the preaching of the pure gospel doctrine (we were then in the month of August, around the time when the Synod of Poissy was held). However, after passing on various teachings to them in his letter, Calvin concluded with these words: 'I warn you and tell you that you will yet have to endure much fiercer battles than you think, for the fury of the wicked knows no bounds...'

He also had a book published in Latin at this time which he entitled *Reply to a coiner...*[4] He wrote this booklet because a man named Francis Baldwin was seeking to gain credence for his views. This man could no more stay in the same place than he could keep to the same religion. He was forever changing his place of residence and his station in life, and he changed his religion at least three times.

Eventually, having no conscience left to lose, he joined an order similar to that of the regular canons. These are in most respects similar to all the other orders, except that they adopt the monastic life in so far as it is to their advantage to do so and, on the other hand, do not regard themselves as bound by the ecclesiastic rule when it does not suit them to live as monks.

So Baldwin kissed the [pope's] slipper like the rest,[5] and so that there should be no doubt that he knew exactly what he was doing, he armed himself with very grand letters patent from the king in order to get back into favour with His Holiness and the cardinals. It has since been his misfortune to become enslaved to them.

So if it is a question of writing against us, he is the most loyal Catholic in the world! But if, on the other hand, it is a question of getting along with those who are, as it were, sitting on the fence and boasting that they keep to the middle of the road, then he comes out with the reformation of the Roman church and brave talk about certain abuses in it. However, Baldwin never gets to the root of the problem, but contents himself with giving the impression to anyone who does not know him that he knows what he is talking about, and that he is not just airing views for the sake of attracting attention to himself.

To begin with, in 1561 he made a point of anonymously publishing a book saying such things at the very time when the conference was being held at Poissy. Calvin, who had realized what this faithless individual was up to, published a reply which, though brief, in his usual style, was very powerful and revealed the character and intentions of this troublemaker for what they were.

Baldwin took exception to this refutation and ever since has continued to vent his spleen against the man whom he had so often hailed as his spiritual father and teacher. This attitude was clear evidence that he had turned against us. Calvin contented himself with maintaining silence by way of reply and of triumphing over the accusations, for he always considered it to be an honour to be the target of personal abuse for the sake of the Lord he served; to say nothing of the fact that to be criticized by a wicked man is in some degree a testimony to one's own good character.

As for the criticisms levelled against his doctrine, Calvin considered these to be so absurd and lacking in substance as not to merit any reply. The rest of Baldwin's allegations simply consisted of a rehash of material borrowed from other sources, which had already been refuted thousands of times.

However, as this apostate persists in pestering me for the gratification of his masters, I have taken the trouble to reply to him a second time, a responsibility which, with God's help, I shall discharge.

Calvin also composed during that same year, as a kind of light relief, a little book called *Congratulations to a venerable priest...* [6] The churchman referred to had the temerity to reprint a book against Luther published some thirty years earlier under the name of King Henry VIII of England. He had introduced this second edition with a preface which he had written himself. However, I am sure he must afterwards have bitten his tongue over this, as Calvin's *Congratulations* certainly took him down a peg or two.

11.
The end approaches

In 1562 Calvin heard of the troubles that were sweeping through the whole of France. He was constantly filled with a great sense of compassion, as if he could see for himself the distress which overtook the churches and the dreadful massacres perpetrated against the poor believers. He was greatly concerned and sought to invoke the use of all lawful means to protect the brethren against the unprecedented violence on the part of the enemies of God, and to restore them to some measure of tranquillity, for the glory of God and the peace of the whole kingdom.

Indeed, besides his private prayers, he took every opportunity to exhort the people publicly to pray to God concerning the great needs of the French churches. On his advice, the syndics and leading men of the town sent the town crier round the city to proclaim, to the sound of a trumpet, a call to everyone to humble themselves before God and to be more diligent in attending public worship. The Christians were asked to gather together, especially on Sundays and on Wednesdays, so that they might pray more fervently to God that he would be pleased to help all the faithful brethren scattered throughout the kingdom of France, and also to pray for the prosperity of the whole country.

It was at about this time that a nobleman who was highly respected in France travelled with his wife through Germany on their way to Lyons and then on to Languedoc. Because of the disturbances which prevailed just about everywhere, they passed through Geneva. There they met Calvin and had discussions with him, which they found most profitable and instructive.

Having concluded his lectures on the prophet Jeremiah on 9 September of this year, Calvin proceeded on 20 September to take the Lamentations of this same prophet. In the course of a conversation on this subject with the other ministers, he said, 'It might be seen as a bad omen for the fate of the churches to speak of "Lamentations", but all things remain in God's hands.' In November, the congregational Bible Study on a Friday began the exposition of the epistle to the Galatians.

The following month, Calvin suffered an attack of gout which lasted several days. This was so severe that on the 18th, which was the day set for the examination of the pastors in preparation for the Christmas communion service, they all gathered in his room while he stayed in bed.

There had been a fierce gale blowing all night long and it continued to increase in fury as the day went on. The wind continued to rage all the next day, which was a Saturday, before dying down on the Sunday. In the presence of the assembled ministers, Calvin remarked on the force of the wind and uttered words which were to prove true in the days that followed. 'I do not know what it is,' he said, 'but all last night, as I listened to this wind, it seemed to me as if I could hear God beating a drum in the breezes. I cannot get the thought out of my mind that something important is happening.' Now, ten or twelve days later, the news reached us that the battle of Dreux had been fought on Saturday, 19 March and, whatever else one may say about it, there is no question that in that battle God rose up against the enemies of his church.

That same year, Calvin wrote the little book entitled *Reply to a Dutchman...*[1] He addressed this work to the believers in the Netherlands. He also drew up the *Confession of Faith of the Reformed Churches in the Kingdom of France.*[2] However, this confession could not reach those for whom it was intended as all routes were blocked because of the war. It was eventually printed in 1564.

In 1563 Calvin was often in very poor health. This is not at all surprising, for as long ago as two or three years earlier it was already obvious that his old health problems were beginning to recur, in particular the migraines and the stomach upsets which caused constant diarrhoea. He also suffered a lot of pain from haemorrhoids, which were all the worse as a result of the trouble he had had in this area seventeen years earlier (as I mentioned)[3] and which had recurred several times since.

These distressing ailments arose from the fact that he allowed his brain so little rest that his digestive system suffered as a result. He was never concerned about his health, except when the pain was so bad that he could no longer disregard it. He was racked with colic pains and then, in the end, a rheumatic form of gout set in.

It is surprising to see how, even in the midst of all these troubles with his health, his mental powers remained as keen as ever, though a little slower to function, and that his skill in judgement was not affected in any way. His only difficulty was that his body had trouble keeping up with his mind, although at times he tried hard to make it do so. As our narrative continues, we shall see this to be the case right up to the day he died.

That year, then, having concluded his lectures on the Lamentations of Jeremiah on 19 January, he began the study of the prophet Ezekiel the very next day. In the weekday sermons, he finished preaching on the first book of Samuel and began the second book on 3 February.

Not long after this he received news from Poland. The false teaching of Stancarus had been unmasked and rejected, but a number of men who indulged in fanciful speculations, including among others George Blandrata, had since been causing trouble among the believers there. These people were seeking to undermine the article of our faith relating to the Trinity, that there are three persons of one divine substance. They were inventing the idea of three distinct natures, and had even gone so far as to draw up a chart showing that the Son and the Holy Spirit are not God in the same way that the Father is.

This led Calvin to publish a *Brief exhortation to the brethren in Poland*. He warned them to beware of making three gods for themselves by inventing three distinct divine natures instead of three persons within the Godhead. This was an attack on the teaching of Matthew Gribaldi and Valentin Gentile. He learnt later that this work had helped many people to understand how cunning these men were, so on the last day of April he wrote a second letter to the brethren in Poland, to strengthen further their belief in this crucial article of our faith.

Calvin also published his *Commentary on the last four books of Moses*, which he compiled in the form of a harmony of the four books. He also had his *Lectures on Jeremiah* printed, which, as I have already said, he had given at the school. In June, an exposition of the book of Joshua was begun during the congregational Bible Study on a Friday.

Towards the end of August, Calvin suffered long periods of acute pain from his gout. These bouts of illness were interspersed with intervals when he was in much less pain, though he was never completely free of it. However, he continued working at home, much as it grieved him that he was unable to fulfil his duties outside. But even when we thought he was resting, he continued to give himself unstintingly to the work. This became very evident to a number of French brethren, ministers of churches there, as they listened to the replies he

Calvin's house on the street in Geneva which now bears his name

gave to the points which they had come to raise with him and discussed the doubts which had arisen in the exercise of their ministry. Calvin received these men very warmly, and although his rheumatic gout restricted his movements, he invited them to his home for a meal at which they were able to meet the other ministers of the church in Geneva, both from the town itself and from the surrounding area.

It was at this time that he translated his commentary on the last four books of Moses, revised the translation of his work on Genesis, and also worked on his commentary on Joshua. He was unable to take part in the September communion service, as his illness forced him to stay at home for almost two months.

When, at last, he began to experience some relief from the attacks of rheumatic gout, he made the effort to go out, sometimes to enjoy the company of friends, but mainly to teach and preach. He had himself carried to the church in a chair. He agreed to conduct the baptismal service for several children.

In mid-January, the other ministers asked him if he would expound the early chapters of Isaiah during the congregational Bible Study on a Friday. On his advice, they had chosen this book to follow on from their study of Joshua.

Dragging himself about in this way, he continued to carry out as many as possible of his public duties until the beginning of February. On Wednesday, the 2nd of this month, he preached his last sermon on the book of Kings. At two o'clock that afternoon he gave his last lecture at the school. This was on Ezekiel. On Sunday, 6 February, he preached his last Sunday sermon on the harmony of the three Gospels.

After that date he never appeared in the pulpit again and most of the time he was obliged to stay at home, without giving any lectures or preaching. Sometimes, however, he still came to church for the congregational Bible Study on a Friday. He ventured to do this as, in all probability, there would be no need for him to speak for an hour at a time, as he had to when giving a lecture or preaching a sermon. On these occasions he would simply add to the message given by the speaker introducing the study whatever God had given him to say about the text which had been expounded. He would also give the exhortation to prayer at the end of the meeting.

The congregation were delighted to have him there. Many people thought that it would be like the other times when he had been ill, and we had seen him recover against all hope, as it seemed. It is true that not only ministers, but friends too, urged him not to wear himself out by coming and working like this. But he would make excuses and say that it did him good and that time would hang too heavily on his hands if he stayed indoors all the time.

However, the illness continued to progress to the point where he was at times so incapacitated that he was barely able to take two or three steps. Yet there were also times when the disease gave him some respite. Although the doctors were doing what they could and he conscientiously followed their advice, he suffered so much pain and so many different illnesses that he could see that it was all in vain.

Looking up to heaven, he would often ask, 'Lord, how long?' He had for a long time taken this phrase as his motto. Eventually, he was forced to stay in bed. He was still able to speak, but he could not keep up a conversation for very long on account of his asthma. However, he continued to work at finishing the books that he had begun to write, which I have already mentioned.

In addition, he continued to take an interest in church affairs, giving answers by word of mouth or in writing as the need arose. We scolded him for not taking more care of his health. His usual reply to this was that he wanted always to be found vigilant and active in God's work to the best of his abilities until he drew his last breath.

On Friday, 1 March, several of the ministers from the church in Geneva, both from the town itself and from the surrounding area, came to visit him after the meal. They found him dressed and sitting at the table. They were alarmed to see that he was very short of breath. Indeed he had to wait a few moments before he was able to speak, and sat supporting his forehead with one hand, as he often did.

When he finally sat up, he looked at them with a gentle expression on his face and said a few words to thank them for their visit and for their concern for him. He told them that he hoped to see the whole company of pastors for one last time in a fortnight's time, which was the date set for their examination in preparation for Easter. 'For,' he said, 'I hope that God will then make clear what is his will for me. I believe that it will be the end of my life, and that he will afterwards take me to himself.'

On Friday, the 24th of the same month, Calvin was much better. All the brethren came to his room for assessment (or examination). He spoke to each one in turn, as was his custom, following the advice given by the brethren, after he himself had first been subjected to an examination by the assembled pastors. The individual assessments took about two and a half hours to complete. Calvin then told the brethren that he felt that God had given him a short stay of execution.

He went on to explain to them some of his doubts about the marginal references which had been included in the New Testament, and told them that he was in the process of revising these comments. Having asked for his papers, he took them and read out long extracts to the assembled company. At his request, they gave him their opinion. As Calvin went on reading, it became obvious that his condition was deteriorating, but as he was enjoying speaking to them, none of the brethren dared urge him to stop reading, especially as they were afraid of upsetting him.

However, the following day it was clear that this occasion had been too much for him, for he was very low in spirits and his health took a turn for the worse. On Monday, 27 March, he had himself carried to the door of the town hall. From there, leaning on those around him for support, he managed to climb the steps to the Council chamber in order to introduce to the leading citizens the man who had been elected as the new head of the school. This meant that the man could take his oath in the presence of the Council, according to the procedure laid down in the school constitution.

When this had been done, Calvin stood up from his seat and, hat in hand, thanked the councillors for the goodwill they had always shown him, and for their kindness to him during his recent illnesses. He went on to say that some days earlier he had felt some improvement in his condition, but that for the last forty-eight hours he had realized that his body could take no more.

He had great difficulty with his breathing as he addressed these words to them in a manner which was so amazingly gracious that it brought tears to the eyes of almost everyone present. That was the last time that he appeared before the Council.

On Sunday, 2 April, the day of the Easter communion service, although he was much weaker, he had himself carried to church in a chair. He was present for the whole sermon and took part in the Lord's Supper. In spite of the difficulties he was having with his breathing, he joined with the others in singing the psalm. You could see from his face how he was rejoicing in the Lord with the whole congregation.

12.
John Calvin's will

On Tuesday, 25 April, Calvin had a very short will drawn up. In fact he had always been in the habit of not wasting words as far as it was in his power to avoid doing so. This will provides a remarkable and valuable testimony to the fact that he remained true to his profession of faith. For this reason, I will reproduce it word for word, with the consent of his brother and sole heir, Antoine Calvin.

This document will thus be preserved for all time, in the same way that it has pleased God that the wills of some of his most worthy servants should be recorded in order to serve as an enduring testimony to the fact that it was the same spirit from God that motivated them both in life and in death.

I also want to show up the sheer impudence of those who try to claim that Calvin's death gave the lie to his life. If anyone accuses me of making things up, I shall not waste time in contradicting him. I will simply advise him, whoever he may be, to reflect on just what would remain certain in human society if doubt could be cast on everything which has been done openly and publicly for all to see or hear who wish to do so.

The last will and testament of John Calvin

In the name of God, Amen. Let it be known and evident to all that in the year 1564, on the 25th day of April, I, Pierre Chenelat, citizen and officially accredited notary of Geneva, was sent for by Mr John Calvin, a minister of the Word of God in the church of Geneva and a burgess of this town, he being ill and indisposed in body, but sound in mind. The above-named person told me that he wanted to draw up his last will and testament and requested me to write it down in the form in which he would dictate and declare it by word of mouth. This I did at his request and wrote it down at his dictation, word for word, without omission or addition in the following form:

In the name of God, I, John Calvin, minister of the Word of God in the church of Geneva, finding myself so afflicted by various illnesses that I am compelled to think that it is the will of God soon to remove me from this world, have decided to set down in writing my last will and testament in the following form.

In the first place, I give thanks to God that, on the one hand, he took pity on me, his poor creature, and brought me up out of the horrible pit of idolatry in which I was plunged in order to draw me into the light of his gospel and make me a partaker of the doctrine of salvation, of which I was quite unworthy. Continuing to show the same mercy to me, he has borne with me through many faults and failings for which I deserved time and time again to be rejected by him.

What is more, he has extended such great mercy towards me that he has been pleased to use me and my labours to teach and make known the truth of his gospel.

I declare that I want to live and die in this faith which he has given me. I have no other hope or refuge than his gracious adoption, which alone is the basis of my salvation.

I gladly receive the grace which he has shown to me in our Lord Jesus Christ and accept the merits of his death and passion as the means by which atonement is made for all my sins. I pray that he will wash and cleanse me by the blood of our great Redeemer, shed for us poor sinners, so that I may appear before him bearing his image.

I also declare that I have sought, according to the measure of grace given to me, to teach his Word in all its purity, whether by sermons or in writing, and faithfully to expound Holy Scripture. Similarly, whenever I have found myself in dispute with the enemies of the truth, I have never used craftiness or acted other than in good faith. On the contrary, I have acted solely in the interests of upholding his Word.

But, alas! my desires and my zeal, if I may so describe it, have been so cold and flagging that I am conscious of imperfections in all that I am and do. If it were not for his infinite goodness, all the affection I have felt would have been no more than a puff of smoke. The very grace that he has shown to me only makes my guilt all the greater — so much so that my only plea is that, since he is the Father of mercies, he may be, and reveal himself as, the Father of such a wretched sinner.

As for the rest, it is my wish that after my decease my body should be buried in the customary way, to await the blessed day of resurrection. Concerning the few worldly goods which God has given me to dispose of, I nominate and appoint as my sole heir my beloved brother, Antoine Calvin. However, I leave him by way of commission only the goblet given to me by M. de

Varannes. I ask him to be content with this, as I am confident that he will be, knowing that the only reason for this request is in order that I may leave the remainder, little as it is, to his children.

Next, I bequeath ten crowns to the college and the same sum to the fund for foreigners in need. Similarly, I bequeath to Jeanne, the daughter of Charles Costans and of my half-sister by my father's side,[1] the sum of ten crowns. Then I leave to Samuel and Jean, my brother's sons and my nephews, forty crowns each. To my nieces, Anne, Suzanne and Dorothée, I leave thirty crowns each. As for my nephew David, their brother, as a punishment for having been heedless and fickle, I give him only twenty-five crowns.

This, then, is the sum total of all the wealth that God has given me, according to what I have been able to calculate and estimate, taking into account my books as well as furniture, crockery and all the rest. However, if there should prove to be more than this, I desire that it should be distributed among my aforementioned nephews and nieces, not excluding David, if, by the grace of God, he learns self-control and adopts a more settled way of life.

But I do not believe that there will be any problem over this point, especially when all my debts have been paid, the responsibility for which I have laid on my brother, in whom I have complete confidence. I hereby appoint him as executor of this will, together with M. Laurent de Normandie. I give them full power and authority to draw up an inventory, without the need for a formal court order to do so, and to sell my furniture in order to raise the money needed to carry out my wishes expressed in the foregoing paragraphs.

Signed and delivered on this 25th day of April.

John Calvin

After I had written it in the form recorded above, Mr John Calvin immediately signed with his own hand and his usual signature this copy of the aforementioned will.

The following day, 26 April 1564, Mr John Calvin summoned me, as well as Messrs Theodore Beza, Raymond Chauvet, Michel Cop, Louis Enoch, Nicholas Colladon, Jacques des Bordes, ministers of the Word of God in this church, and M. Henri Scringer, Professor of Arts, all of them burgesses of Geneva.

In their presence he stated that he had caused me to write at his dictation the aforementioned will, in the form and using the words quoted above. He requested me to read it in his presence and that of the required witnesses who had been requested to attend for that express purpose. I did so and read it aloud, word for word. At the close of this reading he stated that this was indeed his last will and testament and that it was his wish that its provisions should be carried out.

To that effect, he asked the men named above to sign the document with me. This was duly carried out on the date already quoted at Geneva, in the street known as the Rue des Chanoines, and in his place of residence.

In witness whereof, and to serve as such confirmation as may be required to whomever it may concern, I have affixed to the present will in the form set out above, the common seal of our most honoured noblemen and rulers, and my usual signature in my own hand.

Signed as above,

Pierre Chenelat

Since Calvin was growing increasingly short of breath, he sent a message to the four syndics and all the members of the Little Council, as the general council is called, to let them know that he very much wanted to speak to them once more when the Council was in session. With this in view, he said, he would arrange to be taken there on the following Thursday, which was the 27th of the month, to see them all together.

The worthy councillors sent a reply requesting him, in view of his weakness and very poor state of health, not to go to such trouble, but said that they would all come to see him instead. So, on the Thursday morning, they left the Council chamber to go to Calvin's home.

When these men had accordingly all crowded into his room, they exchanged greetings with Calvin. He began by thanking them for being willing to take the trouble of coming to his home, when he had intended to go to the town hall himself.

Then he told them that it had always been his wish to speak to them for one last time. He had not done so earlier, even though there had been several times when his health had been very precarious, because he had not wanted to be too hasty, especially as God had not then given him any indication that his departure was at hand in the way that he was now doing.

After this introduction, he thanked them for having lavished on him more than his due share of honours, and for having supported him on a number of occasions, 'as' he said, 'I know that I was greatly in need of your support'. He regarded himself as being under even greater obligation to them for having always given him so many tokens of their friendship that they really could not have done any more for him.

Although, during his time in Geneva, he had, like all good men, been subjected to much strife and argument, he recognized, however, that the Council had not been responsible for these difficulties.

He went on to say that, if he had not done all that he ought to have done, then he asked them to look at his intentions rather than at what he had actually achieved. He had indeed sought

Addressing the Council for the last time

the good of this town and had made some contribution to that end. He had, however, fallen far short of fully attaining it.

He did not in fact deny that, in the little that he had accomplished, he had been used by God. He would have been a hypocrite if he had said that it was not so. He once more begged his hearers to forgive him for having done so little in comparison with what he ought to have done, both in public and in private life. He considered that the leading men of the city had borne with him even on the occasions when he had been carried away by passion and which he himself deeply regretted. He also had the assurance that God had forgiven him for these outbursts.

He then solemnly declared, in the sight of God and of those assembled to hear him, that he had passed on in all its purity the Word that God had entrusted to him. He had made sure that he did not grope his way forwards blindly or in error. If he had acted otherwise, he would have expected judgement to fall on him. But he was certain that God had been pleased to accept the efforts that he had made to teach people and was with him in these.

He made a point of stressing his conviction of the truth of the doctrine that he had proclaimed to them. He had no doubt that the devil, who constantly tries to pervert or misrepresent the message of the gospel, would raise up in the world evil people with fickle and reckless temperaments who would obey his orders.

He then went on to remind them of the special favours that they had received from God, as well as the grave and pressing dangers from which God had preserved them. He could quote them detailed examples of these things, since he had been in a better position than any to realize the full extent of the dangers that threatened them. He also brought to their attention several things which, according to God's Word, were necessary for the government of the republic.

In short, he acted as a true prophet and servant of God, giving them reassurance in the face of storms still to come, provided that they continued to keep pressing onward in the same direction.

'Consider,' he said, 'the state that you are in. Whether you believe yourselves to be secure, or whether you are threatened by danger, always remember that it is God's will that you should glorify him. He keeps this honour for himself. It is for him to uphold states and their rulers. He wants us to pay homage to him, acknowledging our utter dependence upon him.'

In this connection, he quoted the example of David, who admitted that he had forgotten this truth in a time of security for his kingdom, and who would have fallen never to rise again if God had not had pity on him. 'So then, if a man of such excellent character, of such wealth and power fell,' added Calvin, 'what will become of us, who are nothing?

'We have, therefore, good reason to humble ourselves, and to walk in fear and trembling, taking refuge under the wings of the Almighty, who alone must be the ground of our confidence. However, we may rest assured that, although our security may often seem to hang by a thread, yet God will always continue to watch over us, just as we have already had experience of his deliverance which has taken many different forms.

'If our Lord gives us prosperity, let us take care not to fritter away our time in frivolity and excess, as the unbeliever does. Let us rather give thanks in all humility. When, on the other hand, we are attacked on all sides, and when all around us death threatens us in a hundred different forms, let us still trust in him. So then, every time that dangers or difficulties arise, know that God is calling you to awake and humble yourselves so that you may dwell under the shelter of his wings.

'If you want to keep your freedom, take good care not to abuse the position in which God has placed you. He alone, the

King of kings and Lord of lords, is supreme. He tells us that he will honour those who honour him. On the other hand, he will put to shame those who despise him. He says this in order that you should serve him according to his Word, in all its purity, and that you should go on doing this more and more. Indeed, we fall far short of fully carrying out the task entrusted to us, with the wholehearted commitment it deserves.'

Finally, he addressed them with warnings of a more personal nature. He knew the way of life and the attitudes of almost all of those present, and was therefore well aware that they were in great need of some words of exhortation.

'Even the best of us,' he said, 'is not perfect, but we all have our failings. You should know what they are. Let each one examine himself and seek to conquer his own shortcomings. Some are cold, so wrapped up in their own affairs that they are not concerned for the public good. Others are the slaves of their own passions. There are some to whom God has given intelligence and wisdom, but they fail to make use of them. Others persist in clinging on to their own opinions, wanting to attract attention, and to get a name and influence for themselves.

'Now, those who are older must not be envious of the young for the gifts that they have received. On the contrary, they should rejoice and praise God who is the author of these gifts.

'Let the young retain a sense of modesty without wanting to press too far ahead, for youth always entails an element of boasting, which seeks to exalt oneself and look down on others. Do not discourage one another or stand in one another's way. Avoid offensive behaviour, for the person who is hurt will fly into a rage.

'In order to avoid these evils, let each one of you press on to the best of his ability, faithfully using whatever talents God has given him for the maintenance of this republic. In matters relating to civil or criminal lawsuits, there must be no question of favouritism, hatred, subtle dealings or unlawful patronage. You must give up your own opinions for the sake of maintaining what is right and fair. If you are tempted to adopt a casual attitude, resist the temptation and remain faithful, keeping your eyes fixed on the one who has appointed you. Pray that he will guide you by his Holy Spirit. He will not let you down.'

After saying all that, he begged them once more to forgive him and to make allowances for his infirmities, 'which,' he said, 'I will not deny. Since they are known to God and his angels, I am not ashamed to confess them before men.' He also asked them to accept whatever had been achieved as a result of his efforts in his time among them.

Finally he added these words: 'I pray that our gracious God may continue to guide and govern you, and that he may show you even greater mercies, and turn them to good account for your salvation and that of all this poor nation of ours.'

13.
The last days

On Friday, 28 April 1564, all the pastors from Geneva and the surrounding area were summoned at Calvin's request. They gathered in his room, where he spoke to them at length. The gist of his words was an exhortation to persevere in the faithful discharge of their duties after his death and not to lose heart. God would uphold both the town and the church, even if they were threatened by dangers on every side. There should therefore be no arguments among themselves, but rather brotherly love and a deep sense of unity should prevail.

He also asked them never to forget the obligation that they were under to this church to which God had called them, and to take care that nothing was allowed to distract them from this responsibility. Those who lose interest in the task and want to abandon it will always find excuses to do so, but God will not be mocked.

In this connection, he related the circumstances of how he had come to this church and spoke of the way he had conducted himself among them. When he arrived, the gospel was already being preached, but a very unsettled situation prevailed. For most of the people who lived there, the gospel meant doing away with the old idolatrous practices.

There still remained within the church a number of men who were out to cause trouble, and Calvin had been subjected to numerous indignities. But God had always given him the strength to stand firm, although he was by nature of a rather timid disposition. He repeated two or three times the words: 'I assure you that by nature I am shy and timid.'

He also recalled how he had come back to Geneva from Strasbourg under duress and without any hope of seeing much in the way of fruit as a result of his return. He had no idea of all that God intended to accomplish. In fact, he had still met with numerous difficulties. Yet with time and perseverance, he had seen God's blessing on his labours.

He therefore urged each of his hearers to strengthen himself in the work to which he had been called and to see that everything was well run, watching over the people to keep them obedient to the truth. There were some who were well-disposed to the gospel, but there was also no shortage of troublemakers and rebels. The ministers would have much to answer to God for if, after so much progress had been made, the situation was allowed to deteriorate into a state of disorder as a result of negligence on the part of the shepherds of the flock.

He went on to declare that he had always felt a real affection for all of them as his brothers in the ministry. He begged them to forgive him if at times he had seemed to be out of humour because of his illness. He thanked the brethren, as he had already done on many occasions, for having supported him in his responsibilities by standing in for him when he was unable to preach.

Finally, he shook hands with each of us in turn. We all felt such grief and anguish that I can never recall this scene without feeling extremely sad.

At about this time, a highly respected lady of virtuous character who came from a town of note in France made a special trip to Geneva to see Calvin. She had formerly heard him speaking about the things of God in France, and it was through him that she had come to the knowledge of the truth some thirty years previously. He was very pleased to see her again after such a long time. She would have liked to hear him preach, but seeing this was impossible, had to be content with conversing with him in private, in so far as this was possible in view of his very poor state of health.

Then an old man, who in his youth had been very close to Calvin in the latter's student days, came from the same French town to settle in Geneva. The two men had not seen each other since Calvin left France. Meeting this friend again was another source of great joy to him. However, he did not forget to exhort either of these two who came to see him as to their duty towards God and his gospel. He did so in a plain, unaffected manner, but fervently, zealously and in a way that produced results.

In addition to all this, as a means of simple enjoyment while he waited for God's will for him to come to pass, he invited some of his friends for a meal, both those of Genevan nationality and also foreigners who had taken refuge here for the sake of the gospel. In particular, on one occasion he invited the two people whom I have just mentioned. Nor must I forget to mention the French nobleman who was staying in Geneva at the time and who visited him several times. He even had his meal brought to Calvin's room on one occasion.

On 2 May, after receiving letters from William Farel, the pastor in Neufchatel who has often figured in our narrative and who was now in his eighties, and knowing that this intrepid old man was thinking of coming to see him, Calvin wrote the following letter to him in Latin:

May God bless you, most worthy and very dear brother. Since it is God's will that you should outlive me, keep alive the memory of our fellowship in the work, which has been profitable for the church of God and the fruit of which awaits us in heaven.

I do not want you to tire yourself out on my account. I have great difficulty in breathing and expect at any time to breathe my last. It is enough for me to live and to die in Christ, who is gain to those who belong to him, whether in life or in death.

I commit you to God, you and the brothers who are with you.

I remain wholly yours,
from Geneva, 2 May 1564,
John Calvin.

However, good old Farel did not delay in setting off shortly afterwards to come and see his friend and former fellow-worker. When he arrived in Geneva, the two men conversed and had a meal together, recalling the many years that they had been friends and had worked together in the Lord's service. The next day, Farel preached to the assembled congregation. Then, having taken his leave of Calvin for the last time, he returned to his church at Neufchatel.

From then on until his death, Calvin's time was spent in one long prayer, in spite of his being in constant pain. He often had the words of Psalm 39:9 on his lips: 'I was dumb, I opened not my mouth; because thou didst it.' Or he would quote the words of Isaiah 38:14: 'I did mourn as a dove.' Another time, when he was talking to me, he cried out to God: 'Lord, thou dost grind me to powder, but it is enough for me to know that it is thy hand that does it.'

Many people wanted to come and see him, and his door would have had to be open day and night if they were all to have their wish. Anticipating that this would be the case and conscious that he was growing short of breath, and also to discourage an unhealthy curiosity on the part of some, Calvin had asked that people should content themselves with praying for him and should leave him in peace.

Even when I came to see him, though he always gladly welcomed me because of the responsibility I had taken over, he made it clear that he did not want to see me particularly preoccupied by my concern for him. Sometimes when we took our leave of one another he would tell me that, delighted as he was to see me, he hated giving me all this extra work.

He had always been the type of person who was afraid of doing anything that might hinder the well-being of the church, however slightly, or of causing his friends any worry. They, on the other hand, counted it their chief delight in this world to be able to serve him.

He continued in this state, finding consolation for himself and comforting all his friends, until Friday, 19 May, which was the Friday before the Whitsun communion service. On this day it is customary for all the ministers of this church to come together for a period of self-examination over their conduct and doctrine, before taking a meal together as a token of their friendship.

Calvin agreed that this meal should be held in his home. He had himself carried into the dining room and, on entering the room, said these words to his colleagues: 'My brothers, I come to see you for the last time, for I shall never sit at a table again.' We were all upset by these opening words, although he then went on to lead in prayer as well as his remaining strength would allow and tried very hard to cheer us up.

He only ate very little. Before the end of the meal, he took his leave of us and had himself taken back to his room, which was adjoining the dining room where we were. Putting as brave a face on it as he could, he told us, 'A simple partition will not stop me being one with you in spirit.'

This was indeed the last time that he got up, for up to that time, whatever his state of health, he had always had himself sat at a small table, but after this he stayed in bed because he was so weak. His body was so wasted away that there seemed to be nothing left of him but his spirit. His face, however, had hardly changed at all.

In particular, he was finding it increasingly hard to breathe and was almost choking for breath. Because of this, his prayers and the messages of consolation he was continually uttering resembled sighs more than intelligible words. However, they were accompanied by such a look in his eyes and such a calm expression on his face that his very appearance bore witness to the faith and hope that lived within.

On the day of his passing, Saturday, 27 May 1564, he seemed to regain a little strength and to be more at ease. But it was only nature asserting itself one last time. In fact, that evening, at about eight o'clock, there were suddenly signs that death was very close at hand.

A message was quickly sent to me, when I had only left him a little earlier. I hurried to the house as fast as I could, accompanied by several other brothers, but I found that he had already peacefully breathed his last. He passed away without a word or a groan, or even the slightest movement. He seemed rather to have fallen asleep.

So we see how, at the very same moment that day, the sun set and the greatest light that was in this world for the good of the church of God was taken away to heaven. We can truly say that in this one man God has been pleased to demonstrate to us in our day the way to live well and to die well.

That night and the following day an air of great sadness reigned throughout the town. The people mourned the passing of a prophet of God, and the poor flock were grief-stricken at the loss of their faithful pastor. The school lamented the loss of a true doctor and teacher. Everyone in general wept over a true father and comforter in God.

A number wanted to see his face one last time, as if even in death they could not leave him in peace. Many strangers who had come from afar to see him while he was still alive, but had not been able to because it was not thought that his death was so near, made a great effort to see him, dead as he was.

In order to avoid all this unhealthy curiosity, he was buried the next day, which was Sunday. At about eight o'clock, his body was covered with a shroud and placed in a simple wooden coffin. At about two o'clock, he was taken to the public cemetery called Pleinpalais in the usual way and in accordance with his wishes, without any pomp or ceremony. That is where he still lies today, waiting for the resurrection which had been his constant hope and the theme of his teaching to us. I particularly want to emphasize that everything was carried out in a simple manner, as is customary in our church for the burial of all and sundry.

In fact, several months later, some students who were newly arrived in Geneva were disconcerted when they made a special trip one day to Calvin's grave. They expected to find a magnificent commemorative tomb, but saw nothing there except a burial mound, the same as for all the others. That will at least answer the criticisms of those who have for a long time been accusing us of making an idol of Calvin.

His burial took place in the presence of the syndics and councillors, the pastors of both the French and Italian churches as well as teachers and students. Most of the inhabitants of the town were also present — men and women of every station in life. All will mourn his passing for a long time, especially since there does not seem to be any way of making up such a great loss — at least not in the near future.

I doubt, however, whether we should lament our loss so much as thank God for granting his servant to us for such a long time. In fact, God had put this keen intellect in a weak body, with a tendency to the consumption which would eventually take him from us and which had already been weakened by the long hours of burning the midnight oil when he was young.

In the early days of his ministry, he had so little regard for his health in his devotion to intellectual pursuits that it took a special work of God's grace to preserve the life of this instrument whom God intended to use in the building of his church. Otherwise, it would have been impossible for Calvin even to live to reach what is known as the age of maturity.

On the very day of his funeral, the Queen of England's ambassador to the court of France arrived in Geneva. The court to which he was attached had taken up temporary residence not very far from here, at Dijon. He had therefore taken this opportunity to come and meet Calvin (or so he thought). He was very distressed to see his hopes dashed. Similarly, a French lady of noble birth planned to take advantage of the court's passing through Lyons to visit Calvin, but, as I have already said, he died before the king left Dijon.

Calvin departed this life a month and a half before reaching the age of fifty-five. He spent half of his life in the Christian ministry, both in the spoken word and in writing, without ever changing, adding to, or in any way detracting from the doctrine that he proclaimed on the very first day that he was called to the ministry. He possessed the Spirit of God in such large measure that sinners could never hear him without trembling, nor good men without loving and respecting him.

14.
The elder must be blameless

This, then, is the account of the life and death of John Calvin. Some may have found these pages too long, but, if the truth be told, I must say that I have only written very briefly in comparison with the wealth of material available to us to testify to his good qualities. In fact, if anyone wanted to recount in detail all the important matters in which this man was involved over a period of twenty-three years, in Geneva and elsewhere, there would be enough material to write a very large volume.

Indeed, if ever there was a town or church in this generation that came under a fierce attack from Satan, or that was courageously defended against these assaults, it was Geneva. The glory for its deliverance belongs to God alone, but we can and should say that Calvin was the means he used to make his strength and justice known.

When we consider the vigilance that this man was able to exercise in the course of his ministry, it is a certain fact that he was never caught off guard by Satan or his followers. The enemy never struck a blow but either Calvin had warned the flock of it in advance, or he was able to bring them safely through the battle.

When it comes to his personal integrity, no one was ever able to fault him over the exercise of his pastoral duties. He never let himself be influenced in order to please men, nor was he ever guilty of changing his doctrine or his way of life, or of slandering anyone.

If we consider him from the point of view of his work, I doubt that we could find his equal, for who could tell of all his labours, whether in the normal course of things or for particular situations that arose? I do not know if there is a man alive today who has had to hear, reply to, or write more than he had, or who has been concerned with matters of greater import. The sheer quantity and quality of his writings are enough in themselves to astound even the casual observer, let alone the person who takes the trouble to read them.

The vast amount of work he was able to carry out is all the more remarkable in view of the fact that he possessed a body which was by nature of a delicate tendency and had been weakened by too many late hours and a harshly frugal way of life, and which was prone to so many illnesses. Looking at him, you found it hard to believe that he could live a moment longer.

Despite all this, he never stopped working, night and day, in the Lord's service. He paid no heed to the voices of his friends who daily pleaded with him and urged him to take some rest. Even during his final illness he carried on with his dictation until about a week before his death, even though his voice itself was failing.

In addition to the countless problems associated with his pastoral responsibilities, Calvin also had to bear the even heavier burden of all the dangers and difficulties which threatened this poor city. It was attacked from within by a number of rebels and reckless hotheads, harried from without in a thousand different ways and under constant threat from the most powerful kings and princes of Christendom for giving refuge to and defending the poor children of God who were suffering persecution in France, Italy, Spain, England and elsewhere.

In short, he could well say with the apostle Paul, 'Who is offended, and I burn not?' (2 Corinthians 11:29). People had good reason to seek refuge with him, as God had bestowed on him such a measure of wisdom and discernment that no one was ever any the worse for having followed his advice. On the other hand, I have known all too many who found themselves in extremely difficult situations as a result of disregarding his advice.

I mention only in passing the breadth of his knowledge and his exceptional faculties of judgement. Nor will I stop to dwell on his remarkable affability, which meant that he could meet the very young on their own level when the need arose, nor on the gentleness that he demonstrated in bearing with the weaknesses and failings of others. Indeed I could go on indefinitely if I attempted to speak of all these things.

I will content myself with a reference to his outstandingly good memory. He did not make a show of this, as some, who are more concerned with developing their powers of recollection than those of discernment, have recently tried to claim. Calvin himself was indeed well endowed with both at once, and both in large measure. He also combined these qualities with a very frank and open manner that was totally devoid of affectation.

If someone brought up the subject of particular things that he had witnessed in the past, whether in France, Italy or Germany, he would be able to talk about them, mentioning people and places by name and turning the discussion to good account.

When it was a question of the affairs of the church in Geneva, indeed, insofar as his calling made this possible, of the republic itself, his knowledge appeared to cover every aspect of the subject and extended to matters of minute detail.

On occasions when the consistory was in session and particular individuals were summoned to appear before it to answer for fresh misdemeanours, he would remember their previous appearances, giving the reasons and causes of each. And if anyone took the trouble to consult the records of the consistory's proceedings he would find that Calvin had been right in every detail, even if the event had occurred seven, ten or even twelve years earlier.

It was the same in matters of doctrine and history, as all who have listened attentively to him, and all those who were on close terms of intimacy with him, know very well. When he gave his lectures he never had anything in front of him other than simply the words of Scripture. Yet we can see that his teaching was presented in an orderly manner.

When he gave his lectures on Daniel a few years before his death, despite the fact that at certain points he needed to refer to a wealth of historical detail, he did not use a single note to jog his memory.

It was not that he spent a long time preparing his lectures beforehand. He would not have had the time to do this if he had wanted to. If the truth be told, he often had less than an hour in which to prepare. But his mind was so alert that he could grasp at once the sense of what he was reading, instantly formulate a sound judgement on the subject and accurately remember the whole.

I will add one other testimony to his powers of memory which was an everyday occurrence. If someone came to talk to him while he was in the middle of dictating, even if the interruption lasted for an hour, more often than not he could remember the point at which he had stopped. He would then carry on with what he had been saying without even looking at what had gone before — whether he was composing a letter or working on a commentary.

As far as his daily life is concerned, everyone will testify to the fact that he never lapsed either into over-indulgence or stinginess, but maintained a commendable balance between the two. It is true that because of his gastric troubles he abstained from eating certain common foods that he would otherwise have liked. But he was not being fussy in avoiding these foods nor did he make things difficult for those around him.

He was guilty, however, of failing to take proper care of his health. For many years he made do with just one meal a day, going all day long without ever having anything else. It was only six months before his final illness that his doctors managed to persuade him to drink a little wine occasionally and to swallow a raw egg at midday.

The reason for this abstemiousness lay in his stomach troubles and migraines. He said he had found that the only thing which helped was a very strict diet all the time. I have also known him sometimes go without food for forty-eight hours. Leading the kind of life he did, he also slept very little. However weary he was as a result of all this, he never failed to be ready for work or for carrying out his responsibilities.

The days that he was not preaching, at about five or six o'clock in the morning he would have some books brought to his bed so that he could prepare his writings, which he then dictated to a secretary. If it was his week to preach, he was always ready when it was time to go into the pulpit. When he returned home, he would go to bed or lie down fully dressed and would continue his work with the help of a book.

He found that lying down helped with the treatment of his gastric troubles. With the same object in view, he would often have several changes of warm linen. This was how he spent his mornings, devoting them to the dictation of most of his books, since he saw this as the time of day when his mind worked most efficiently.

We can see, then, the kind of life led by this worthy servant of God. He would forget himself in order that he might serve God and his neighbour in the work to which he had been called

Calvin at his books

and appointed. Nor do I want to pass over in silence the fact that, in spite of all his hard work, Satan levelled against him all kinds of slanderous accusations with the greatest effrontery in the world. There is nothing new in this, for that is the way the world has always seen fit to repay those who want to save it from perdition.

Simply reading the account of Calvin's life is enough to refute the charges made against him. In fact, I will confine myself to mentioning just a few points that will enable the truth to be seen and understood clearly.

Charges levelled against Calvin

He was a heretic

Some people attached this label to him, even going so far as to coin the new name of 'Calvinists'. But I beg you to tell me whether the doctrine to which he bore faithful witness for many years, right up till the time of his death, both in writing and by the spoken word, is not in itself more than sufficient to rebut this accusation?

Has anyone read in his writings, heard in his preaching, or seen in his conduct anything that tends towards heresy? On the contrary, do not these three aspects of his life demonstrate that this man only ever spoke of the Word of God in all its purity and in accordance with divine revelation?

We may say that he taught true godliness to others, essentially like that which he cherished in his own heart, and that was all that he desired to do. Ambition has long been called the mother of all heresies. If anyone can put forward one single argument to prove that Calvin entertained an ambitious spirit, then I would agree to his being labelled a heretic.

Was there ever a man who expounded the Bible in a more straightforward manner, or who would have been more capable of drawing attention to himself, had he wished so to do, by a misuse of Scripture and dabbling in niceties of interpretation or futile displays of erudition?

It is true that many people rejected his doctrine. But this fact alone is not sufficient grounds for people of sound judgement to regard him as suspect. On the contrary, this point could in itself be used as an argument in his favour, especially since no one ever opposed him without discovering that he was confronting not just a mere man but a true servant of God. So we may say (and all who knew him will provide adequate confirmation of this) that no enemy ever attacked him without also waging war against God himself.

We might well say that, ever since God first caused this champion to enter the lists to fight for his cause, Satan has singled him out as a target, as if he had forgotten the existence of all the others in order to attack this one man and if possible vanquish him. However, God graciously bestowed on him the honour of gaining as many victories as he caused there to be adversaries ranged against him.

I declare, then, that his doctrine was sound, pure and holy, and his teaching methods were characterized by sincerity and openness, yet at the same time they carried authority and proved effective. I might add that those who sought to decry or discredit his teaching succeeded only in confirming and providing further proof of the very truths they were attempting to undermine. This was true both of those opponents who were present on the spot and of those who attacked him from a distance.

Indeed, these assailants were not able to attack from so great a distance that Calvin's reply did not touch them much more nearly than they would have liked. Anyone can confirm that this is so from a simple examination of the principal battles that he had to fight on behalf of the doctrines which have already been mentioned in the course of our narrative.

The case of the Anabaptists who came to attack him shortly after he began his ministry in Geneva attests this fact. It was the same for the apostate Caroli, who accused Calvin, Farel and Viret of Arianism.[1] Or again, what did the noble Cardinal Sadoleto achieve in taking Calvin on, except to find himself effectively silenced by the latter? Or what can I say about Pighius, that Goliath of a man whose Pelagianism was brought crashing down by the Lord's power through the hand of his servant? It is also appropriate to mention here Calvin's scholarly writings against the Anabaptists and the Libertines.

Has there ever been a man who was more perceptive in detecting and rejecting the ungodliness of those false evangelicals who try to please everybody and call themselves Nicodemites? Who ever fought more effectively to drive off all the wild boars that gathered to lay waste the Lord's vineyard? Who has done more to thwart the designs of Antichrist? Who replied more courageously or with greater relevance to that notorious *Interim* that has caused so much trouble in Germany?[2]

Is it possible to give a better reply than Calvin did to all the arguments of those who oppose the holy doctrine of predestination and of God's eternal providence — truths which the ungodly Bolsec had misrepresented in that monk's head of his? Or what can I say about the battles that Calvin engaged in to defend the divinity and eternal existence of the Son of God against the attacks of Servetus, Valentin Gentile and the others who followed them at that time?

Or again, who was more vigorous in defending the purity of the doctrine in the face of the very dangerous adversaries that those clever men whom he referred to as 'coiners' proved to be? On the pretext of wanting to bring about peace and unity, these men aspired to corrupt the truth in their attempts to win the approval of men and to further their own interests.

Finally, what benefit did those stubborn characters Joachim Westphal and Tileman Hesshusius reap from all their efforts, beyond showing themselves up as the bitterest enemies of truth and harmony that anyone has ever seen? For, when they forced Calvin into a confrontation, he was so successful in upholding the truth and in combating the ignorance and the sheer impudence of these individuals that he won all the praise and they were put to shame, even among members of their own sect and people of their own nationality. The church of God, on the other hand, came out of it confirmed in their stand for this true and holy doctrine.

To sum up, I believe that there is not a heresy to be found, whether an old one, or one that has been revived or newly invented, that Calvin did not destroy to its very foundations. Among his other excellent qualities two particularly stood out — a remarkable ability to penetrate to the very root of a problem, and an amazing skill in setting out his reply using the fewest possible number of words. All who examine his writings carefully, even those who are opposed to the gospel, will recognize that this is the case.

He wanted to be in charge of everything

There are some who make such a claim. What a brazen and hideous lie! What is this pre-eminence that he is supposed to have sought, for if such had been his wish, who could have prevented him from obtaining it? When did he ever engage in a debate with anyone to decide who would be in charge? Did he change his way of life because he had been accorded the respect which was due to the gifts and qualities with which God had endowed him?

When did anyone ever see him abuse his position or his authority even in relation to the very least and lowest? When did he ever embark on any project without consulting his colleagues in the ministry, or against their advice? Even when he came to the end of a series of sermons or lectures on a book of Scripture, although he knew better than anyone else what would be most suitable and most useful for the building up of the church, he never started on a new series without first asking the other ministers for their advice.

In short, in what way was he any different from the rest of us, except that he surpassed all of us in humility and went to a lot more trouble than any of us? Not only did he discharge his duties faithfully, but he did so very courageously and honourably, yet without drawing attention to himself, or even appearing to do so.

As a result of the powerful work of God in his heart and life, we may say that, as far as this can be said of any Christian in this life, Calvin was a man who was humble but not lacking in courage, magnanimous but not proud.

He was a spendthrift and a gambler

People have accused him of this, but without any grounds for doing so. For was there ever a man who dressed more simply, or whose whole attitude displayed greater modesty? Did any man of his station in life ever have a house that was, not more sumptuously, but more poorly furnished than his? If people are not prepared to take my word for it, or that of ten thousand witnesses besides, the small income enjoyed by his brother, who was his sole heir, and the inventory of all his possessions, will demonstrate the truth of this.

When it came to games of chance, it is true that sometimes, in appropriate circumstances and within the circle of his close friends, he would relax by joining in a game of tossing a disc or a key[3] or any other legitimate game that is not forbidden in this republic. He did so only very rarely, and then rather in response to the urging of his friends than on his own initiative.

Normally, in addition to the time he spent working on his books and studying, which kept him occupied for the rest of the day, he would take a short rest for a quarter of an hour following the meal, or half an hour if someone else was with him, before returning to his desk.

As for those who accused him of wastefulness and all that such a failing entails, I answer that, at the very least, his books will bear witness until the end of the world to the way he spent his time and will show up these people for the barefaced liars that they are.

Calvin was a miser

Others, on the contrary, accused him of being miserly, some even going so far in shamelessly maligning him as to claim that he was guilty of usury. They gave him the nickname of 'the banker' — a totally ridiculous and completely unfounded charge, a blatant lie which anyone who knew him, however slightly, will easily be able to disprove. As he himself wrote somewhere, if there were people who could not rid themselves during his lifetime of the notion that he was rich and in possession of a large fortune, they would be disabused of this idea after his death when the inventory of his possessions was drawn up.

Anyone who examines this will find that the total value of his estate (including his library, which fetched a good price at the sale because of the value attached to the memory of its owner) did not exceed two hundred crowns. It is true that by his own reckoning he was not poor, because his expenditure did not exceed his income.

As far as the charge of avarice is concerned, he had so much of it that when he found that he had been awarded a salary of six hundred florins (which is no more than three hundred pounds in the currency of Tours),[4] he asked that he might receive less, as the leading men of the town can testify. He was so covetous of this world's goods that, highly regarded as he was, and even honoured, by the princes and noblemen of many nations, and even though he had dedicated his works to them, I doubt whether he received even as much as twenty crowns from their patronage (and I would have known if that had been the case).

He had such a respect for the Word of God that he would rather have died than make use of it as an enticement to further his own ambition or avarice. He dedicated many of his books to particular people to thank them for some act of kindness, or simply as a mark of friendship.

For example, as I mentioned in an earlier chapter, he dedicated his book on Seneca to one of the lords of Montmor, in whose company he had been educated during his student days in Paris. He dedicated his commentary on the epistle to the Romans to Simon Grynaeus[5] and that on 1 Corinthians to the noble marquis Caracciolo. His commentary on 2 Corinthians was dedicated to Melchior Volmar, who taught him Greek, the one on 1 Thessalonians to Mathurin Cordier, who had formerly been his teacher at the school in Paris, that on 2 Thessalonians to his doctor, Benedict Textor, and that on the epistle to Titus to his two old friends and fellow-workers in the Lord's service, William Farel and Pierre Viret. His book on scandals was addressed to his lifelong friend Laurent de Normandie. Forty of his other works were dedicated to various kings, princes, or republics, with the aim of encouraging them by this means to persevere in protecting the children of God, or to incite the others to do so.

If, on the other hand, he saw that the person in question was doing the exact opposite, or was quite indifferent to his labours, then he would not hesitate to remove that person's name and replace it with another. However, this only happened on two or three occasions.

Calvin lived a life of debauchery

Some even had the effrontery to slander him with accusations of this kind.[6] We might be surprised that such a blatant lie should raise its head, were it not for the fact that the world has a habit of treating God's most eminent servants in this way. Yet not one of his fellow-citizens ever entertained even the slightest suspicion that the man we are speaking of was guilty of this particular failing.

He was married for about nine years, with all regard for the sanctity of the marriage relationship. After his wife's death, he remained a widower for the sixteen years which remained until his own death. During all that time, who ever noticed the slightest evidence of such a shameful blot on his character as this of which certain people are accusing him? What woman would have been so evil and shameless as to dare even to think of casting an immodest glance in the direction of one who always presented such a venerable and upright appearance to all those around him? Who ever fought more vigorously against all forms of debauchery than Calvin?

It is true that the Lord tested him in the case of some who were very close to him.[7] Worse things than those to which I am alluding took place in the family of Jacob, or in that of David. But what did Satan gain from all this in regard to this faithful servant of God, except shame and disgrace — for himself when he appears before the judgement seat of the Son of God on the last day, and even now for those enticed by him into giving him occasion for speaking reproachfully?

These unhappy people regard bawdiness, adultery and incest as harmless indulgences or subjects for entertainment. They consider it highly outrageous that the reformed churches should punish those guilty of debauchery and adultery. If scandals were to arise among us, even though they would be severely punished, these people would not hesitate to point the finger at us. Even if they were telling the truth in making such charges, they would only be accusing us of being like them.

But let us not waste too many words on this subject. Whether they like it or not, they will have to admit that bandits do not gather around the gallows. Those who commit such misdemeanours prefer to meet where crime is regarded as a virtue.

To return to what I was saying, you will find that this faithful servant of God set a remarkable example to men the whole world over by his condemnation of such wicked and disgusting vices, whether among Christians or others. If anyone was found guilty of such things, Calvin never showed partiality to anyone. He only had regard for God and his church. In saying this I am not putting forward anything, the truth of which is not vouched for in the sight of God by all.

Calvin was short-tempered, cruel and even bloodthirsty

Some people have spoken of him in these terms. Others, wanting to tone down these accusations, settled for describing him as being too strict. It is not at all difficult, thank God, to defend him. It would not even be necessary to do so, were it not that some need to be reproved for their waywardness and others for their ingratitude towards God.

I repeat once again what I said at the beginning, namely, that his only enemies were either those who did not know him or those who were openly waging war against God. I shall cite one piece of evidence in support of this statement which will be more than adequate to prove my point.

Indeed, we would be hard-pressed to find in our day a man of his station in life against whom Satan has waged a more gruelling war by every kind of slanderous attack. Yet, for all that, we do not find Calvin frequenting the courts of justice or spending his time consulting lawyers, still less seeking to take any kind of revenge. He never had a house or an inheritance to defend, and he never meddled with trade or commerce.

It is true that when opposition arose against the doctrine of God that he proclaimed, he was not diverted from his course but brought proceedings against the mockers, in accordance with the righteous laws of the republic, so that they should reap the fruits of their wrongdoing. But who will find fault with him for doing that, except those who want to turn one of the rarest and most precious virtues into a destructive vice which is all too common?

Besides, what conclusion can we come to if I say — as I can in all truth — that a number of those whom he had to oppose for the reasons I have mentioned were themselves to testify to his faithfulness?

I will mention three such cases, without giving names. Two of them, who were going to bear the punishment due to their crimes, could not refrain, in full view of everyone, from honouring him and expressing their gratitude to him right up to the end. They called him their father and cried out that they were unworthy of his attendance, or of his warnings and prayers, for they had not heeded his fatherly words of exhortation. The third, who had acted as a counsellor to all those who led lives of debauchery, could not be convinced, as he lay on his death-bed, that God had forgiven him unless the faithful servant of God whom he had offended so much would forgive him too. These three, at least, did not accuse Calvin of cruelty, or of being too strict.

I admit that he always told the magistrates how much God detests favouritism, and that he showed them the importance of judging impartially. He used to tell them that those who condemn the innocent were an abomination in the sight of God, just as much as those who acquit the guilty. If it is a crime to speak and act in such a way, then we would have to condemn the Holy Spirit, who inspired these things in the Word of God. If the opposite is true, then the blasphemers who describe what God has ordained as cruel should keep their mouths shut.

But, someone may say, Calvin was too strict towards adulterers and heretics. To this I will reply that in fact, as the whole town knows, he never passed judgement on anyone, nor ever had any thought of doing so, as that was not his responsibility. It therefore has to be said that even when his advice was sought — not with the intention of confusing the roles that God has decreed should be kept separate, but in order to be guided by the precepts of the Word of God — it was not always followed.

But enough of that. What will be the reply of our critics, who are so ready to show mercy, if I point out that there has in fact never been a well-ordered republic in which adultery was not deemed a crime worthy of death? And yet you will not find in this city a single case of an adulterer being sentenced to capital punishment.

And when it comes to heretics, where, I should like to know, do we find examples of this excessive severity they accuse him of? In what instances did this bloodthirsty character that they make Calvin out to be ever reveal his natural inclination for shedding blood? There are very few towns in Switzerland or Germany in which Anabaptists have not been put to death, and with good reason. Here, they were merely banished.

Bolsec blasphemed against the providence of God in this city. Sebastian Castellio poured scorn on the very books of Holy Scripture here. Valentin Gentile blasphemed against the Godhead here. Not one of those men died here. The first two were simply banished, and the third was let off on the condition that he made amends in the sight of God and the leading men of the town. So where is all this cruelty?

But what about Servetus?

He alone was burnt at the stake. And was there ever anyone
more deserving of such a fate than that wretched man? Over a
period of thirty years, he was guilty of many different kinds of
blasphemy against the doctrine of the eternal existence of the
Son of God. He gave to the Trinity of three persons in one
divine substance the name of 'Cerberus'. He denied the
baptism of infants and his teaching was a hotch-potch of most
of the countless perversions of God's truth that Satan has ever
come up with.

Servetus led many people astray. To crown it all, he refused
to repent or to give any reason to hope that he might change and
accept the truth by which he had been shown on so many
occasions to be in the wrong.

Or what about the verdict of the churches? Should we not
take into account what was said about Servetus by all the
German churches, and notably by Philip Melanchthon, who
was so renowned for his gentleness? The latter was not content
with speaking on the subject, but also put in writing his
approval of an execution which was so clearly justified.

Finally, before we leave this subject, those who believe
such an act to be wrong display only too clearly their own
ignorance in finding fault with something which met with such
a remarkable degree of approval, and their foolhardiness in
attacking Calvin. He was only acting as a faithful pastor,
instructing the magistrates in their duty, trying by every possible means to bring a wretched sinner to change his ways and,
ultimately, to leave no stone unturned for the sake of protecting his flock from being infected with such evil doctrine.

Calvin was quick-tempered

Some have accused Calvin of being short-tempered. I do not
want to make this man out to be an angel. However, I cannot

fail to mention the remarkable extent to which God made use of the very forcefulness of his character. I want in all honesty to take all the circumstances into consideration. Besides a temperament that was by nature prone to anger, there were a number of things that tended to make him irritable and difficult to get on with.

These included, for example, his own lively mind, the lack of discretion on the part of many of those around him, and the many and varied affairs he had to deal with concerning the church of God. Towards the end of his life, the many illnesses and infirmities to which he was subject also came to be added to this list. But he was far from seeking to make excuses for this failing. On the contrary, no one was more aware of it, or more conscious of its importance, than he was himself.

Having said all that, this was the only fault that I ever saw evidence of in his private life or conduct. It was tempered by many fine qualities, and was accompanied by few, if any, of the other shortcomings that so often result from this particular failing. This was true to such an extent that not one of his friends suffered any lasting offence as a result of anything that he did or said.

When we come to his public life and the responsibilities entrusted to him by God, I can only wonder at the great wisdom of God, who overrules all things for his own glory, especially in the case of those whom he wants to use in a more particular way.

Those who have seen and known for themselves the type of people that Calvin had to deal with more often than not, and all that God made known and brought about through him, as well as the particular circumstances of the times and places in which he lived, are those who are in a position to judge to what extent such forcefulness of character — truly prophetic in its proportions — has been of service, and will continue to be of service for generations to come.

Calvin rejected every expedient of those who seek to inspire fear by their outward appearance. However, it is all the more remarkable that even the most stubborn and perverse of men were obliged to yield before the aura of great authority with which God had surrounded his faithful and blameless servant.

The reader who is truly seeking the glory of God will see this sense of majesty of which I am speaking permeating Calvin's writings. There are those today who treat religion like questions of politics, people who are colder than ice towards the things of God, yet more ardent than fire where their own interests are concerned. Anything that is said with more frankness than they would like they call anger. Calvin never tried to please such people, but I will pause for a moment to address them. What would these people, who think themselves so wise and so sensible, say if they had come into closer contact with such anger? I am sure that they would have complained about it. For my own part, as long as I live I will consider myself privileged to have had a taste of so noble and rare a quality in both public and private life.

In closing, I declare that I will indeed never tire of consoling myself for the absence of such a fine man by recalling the rare and delightful qualities that he possessed. Although I can never think of his death without a deep sense of grief, yet I take great comfort in thinking of it as in a very real sense the crowning glory of his whole life.

Since it has pleased God that Calvin should continue to speak to us through his writings, which are so scholarly and full of godliness, it is up to future generations to go on listening to him until the end of the world, so that they might see our God as he truly is and live and reign with him for all eternity. Amen.

Written from Geneva, 19 August 1564.

Notes

Chapter 1 — The early years

1. The Montmor family were related to the bishop of Noyon. Gérard Calvin, who was for a time the bishop's secretary, arranged for his son to join the children of this family in their lessons with their private tutor. John Calvin arrived in Paris in August 1523, and went to stay in the home of his uncle, Richard Calvin, who was a locksmith.

2. The post was that of chaplain in the la Grésine (i.e. Nativity) Chapel of Noyon Cathedral. Calvin was only twelve when he was appointed to the post and he continued to hold it during his time in Paris. It was not unusual at that time for young boys to be appointed to office in the church. Odet de Châtillon, brother of the famous Admiral Coligny who was killed in the Massacre of St Bartholomew's Day, became a cardinal at the age of sixteen!

3. Calvin was appointed parish priest of Marteville at eighteen years of age. Two years later he switched positions with the priest of Pont-l'Evêque. He did not renounce these ecclesiastical offices until 1534.

4. This name, which began as a nickname, but which he came to adopt as a surname, referred to his habit of 'burning the midnight oil' in his student days.

5. In the preface to his commentary on the Psalms, Calvin himself records that, in the year following his conversion, all those who were seeking a purer form of doctrine were constantly coming to him for instruction. However, he was then, to use his own words, 'only a novice and an apprentice'.

Chapter 2 — The road to Geneva

1. 'His memory', he says, 'should be held in honour among the faithful, for he was a holy martyr for Christ.'

2. Du Tillet was canon of Angoulême and parish priest of Claix. He later reverted to Roman Catholicism.

3. Servetus had just published his book denying the Trinity.

4. At that time, Francis I needed to form an alliance with the German Protestants in order to rise up against the Holy Roman Emperor, Charles V. He therefore sought to persuade the Lutheran princes that those who were burnt at the stake in Paris were not Protestants but a few survivors of the fanatical extremists who had caused so much trouble in Germany.

5. Renée de France, the daughter of Louis XII and cousin of Marguerite de Navarre. In later years her castle at Montargis became a refuge for persecuted Protestants.

6. He was also accompanied by his sister Marie, of whom little is known beyond the reference in Calvin's will to her husband and daughter. Antoine was a bookbinder. He later became a citizen of Geneva and served on two of the city councils. He died in 1573.

Chapter 3 — Early conflicts lead to expulsion from Geneva
1. Caroli falsely accused Calvin of denying the deity of Christ.
2. On Easter Sunday, Calvin and Farel had declared that they would not celebrate communion in a town where there was so much in the way of excess, arrogance and debauchery. The next day they received orders to leave the republic's territory.
3. The highest office in the republic of Geneva. There were four syndics who were elected on an annual basis.
4. Calvin married Idelette de Bure in September 1539. A son was born to the couple in 1542 but he lived only a short time. Idelette already had two children by her first marriage and Calvin acted as a father to them. Idelette never fully recovered her health after the birth of their son and died in 1549.
5. This is the only poetry that Calvin had published.

Chapter 4 — Back to Geneva
1. The Great Council voted on 2 January 1542 to adopt on a permanent basis the code of church discipline and practice drawn up by Calvin.
2. Versions also existed in Hungarian, Basque and Polish.
3. Wolfgang Capito, an intimate friend of Bucer and other leading Reformers, died of the plague in 1541.

Chapter 5 — Calvin's writings up to 1549
1. Albert Pighius of Kampen (1490-1542) stood out as one involved in all the theological debates of the time. He was a staunch defender of Roman Catholicism and opposed the Reformers, especially Bucer and Calvin.
2. There were some believers in France who had submitted to Roman Catholicism because they were afraid of persecution. They subsequently justified the position they had taken by claiming that they maintained a purity of heart.
3. A Franciscan who had embraced the false teaching of the free-thinkers and who was at that time causing trouble in this church by spreading the errors of Carpocratus, a second-century teacher who proclaimed a message characterized by syncretism (the attempt to reconcile opposed systems of belief) and licentiousness.
4. The *Interim* was a system of doctrine thought up by Charles V in 1548, in order to bring about a reunion between the Catholics and Protestants in Germany. Three theologians, of whom one was a Protestant, drew up the articles of faith, but both sides rejected this attempt at compromise. Charles V himself abandoned it four years later following the treaty of Passau.

Chapter 6 — Consolidating the work
1. The event referred to was one of the disturbances engineered by the faction led by Ami Perrin and his wife, who before her marriage was Françoise Favre. In earlier days, Perrin had acted to protect Calvin and had been a member of the delegation that brought him back from Strasbourg. It would seem that the influence of his wife and her family caused him to turn against Calvin and become a leading voice among the opponents of reform.
2. Perrin and his supporters were trying to transfer the responsibility for the exercise of church discipline from the consistory to the Council.
3. In 1554 there were estimated to be more than 1,300 refugees who had settled in Geneva.

4. Wolfgang Musculus, one of the most famous Hebrew scholars of his age, was the son of a cooper. At the age of fifteen he entered a Benedictine monastery, but soon left because of his views. He was subsequently forced by poverty to take up weaving, and later to work as an unskilled labourer on the construction of the fortifications of Strasbourg. Bucer employed his skills as a copyist. He began the study of Greek and Arabic at the age of forty.

5. 'Truly mine is no common grief,' he wrote to Viret at that time. 'I have been bereaved of the best friend of my life, of one who, if it had been so ordained, would willingly have shared not only my poverty but also my death. During her life she was the faithful helper of my ministry. From her I never experienced the slightest hindrance' (Quoted by T. H. L. Parker, *John Calvin,* Lion Publishing, 1975, from the *English Translation of Calvin's Letters,* 2, 202).

6. Graubünden (or the Grisons) is now one of the Swiss cantons.

7. Martin Bucer had been summoned to England by Cranmer, the Archbishop of Canterbury, and continued to teach there until his death. In the reign of Queen Mary, his body was exhumed and burnt, but Elizabeth I had a monument erected in his memory.

Chapter 7 — Under fire from Satan

1. Valla was one of the most eminent philosophers of the fifteenth century. He wrote against the mystery of the Trinity, and in defence of free will, among other things. The Inquisition condemned him to be burnt at the stake, but the sentence was never carried out.

2. Jerome Hermes Bolsec was chaplain to the Duchess of Ferrara when he became a Protestant. After his expulsion from Geneva, he reverted to Catholicism. He later published two vitriolic pamphlets attacking Calvin and Beza, but it is generally accepted that these are the work of a bitter man seeking revenge on his opponents and are of no historical value.

3. Beza himself also published a short book on the subject in which he attempts to justify the judges who condemned Servetus. The errors propagated by Servetus did not in fact all die with him. A number of the views that he put forward were to resurface later.

4. This refers to a man named Philibert Berthelier. He and his brother François-Daniel, the sons of a Genevan hero and martyr for freedom, belonged to the group that was systematically opposing Calvin. Philibert had been excluded from the Lord's Table since 1551.

Chapter 8 — The sword and the trowel

1. This is proved by the reception he gave to Valentin Gentile on his arrival in Berne (see chapter 9 for more about Gentile).

2. The full title of this work is: *Reforms to silence a certain knave named Antoine Cathelan, formerly a Franciscan at Albigeois.*

Chapter 9 — Keeping up the good fight

1. Pelagius denied the doctrine of original sin and the need for God's grace.

2. At the time that Beza was writing, Sebastian Castellio had just died of the plague in Basle.

Chapter 10 — Treasure in earthen vessels

1. Up till 1549, Nicolas des Gallars had written down the outlines of Calvin's lectures and filled in the detail afterwards. He would then read the whole out aloud to Calvin and make any corrections required by the Reformer.

2. King Henry III wanted to reinstate the Duke of Savoy and do away completely with the state of Geneva.

3. Francis Stancarus, from Mantua, was a professor of Hebrew first in Krakow and later in Königsberg. He died in Stobnitz in 1574. He maintained that Jesus Christ had only redeemed us *as a man*. 'For,' he said, 'if he had been mediator *as God*, far from being co-essential with God, he would only be of a secondary divine nature.'

4. *Reply to a certain crafty coiner who, while pretending to be providing the means for reconciliation, is attempting to thwart and turn aside the progress of the gospel in the kingdom of France.* Baldwin was given the nickname Ecebodius ('Changeable'), as he wavered between religions as the indecisive man that he was.

5. Kissing the pope's slipper was a gesture of penitence on behalf of a 'heretic' when he was once more received into favour by the pontiff.

6. *Congratulations to the venerable priest, M. Gabriel de Saconay, the principal cantor of the church in Lyons, on the beautiful little preface with which he adorned the King of England's book.* This Gabriel de Saconay, who died in 1580, is known only because of the vehemence of his writings opposing the Reformation.

Chapter 11 — The end approaches

1. The full title was *Reply to a Dutchman who, under the guise of making Christians totally spiritual, allows them to pollute their bodies with all kinds of idolatry*.

2. Calvin wrote this confession of faith on behalf of the Prince of Condé and all the faithful believers in France. He intended to present it to the emperor and the princes of the German states when they met in Frankfurt.

3. See chapter 6.

Chapter 12 — John Calvin's will

1. Marie Calvin was the daughter of Gérard Calvin by a second marriage. She followed her brothers John and Antoine to Geneva (see chapter 2, note 6).

Chapter 14 — The elder must be blameless

1. Arius denied the deity of Christ.

2. See chapter 5, note 4.

3. Rabelais spoke of this game, which appears to have consisted of throwing a key onto a table and seeing who could get nearest to the edge.

4. Currency minted at Tours was considered to be one quarter less in value than that minted in Paris.

5. Simon Grynaeus taught first Greek and later theology. We owe the discovery of the last five books of Livy to him.

6. Bolsec's book includes a chapter headed 'Calvin's impurity and lust'.

7. In 1557 his brother Antoine's wife, Anne de Fer, the daughter of a refugee from Arras, was found guilty of adultery, and Antoine obtained a divorce. Some time later Calvin's step-daughter Judith was also convicted of adultery (Parker, *John Calvin*, p.121).